A LIFE OF RHYME

A Poetic Life-Commentary

Pascal Rowland

ARTHUR H. STOCKWELL LTD
Torrs Park, Ilfracombe, Devon, EX34 8BA
Established 1898
www.ahstockwell.co.uk

DEDICATION

To Angie
We exist through the recognition of others . . .

ISBN 978-0-7223-4933-5
Printed in Great Britain by
Arthur H. Stockwell Ltd
Torrs Park   Ilfracombe
Devon EX34 8BA

SONNET TO ORIGINATION

Why do we never elicit suggestions
When we go knocking at the door
With myriad perplexing questions
About love, hate, death and war?

Perhaps the art of living this puzzling life
Is to domicile ourselves to our inner mind,
And try to be happy and forget the strife,
And possibly then satisfaction we'll find.

So be careful and cautious in each decision,
For it's likely that we only have one show;
Unless there's a God and He'll make His revision,
And commend or condemn as to where we go.

That is if you believe in an afterworld,
But only death will leave the answer unfurled.

SONNET TO UNCERTAINTY

All over the world people altercate
And in families, parents their children berate,
Very often for no particular cause
Except to uphold our social mores.

Everywhere there are people who are opulent,
As well as people who are despondent,
Indolent, industrious and penurious
And obsequious, arrogant and nefarious.

These are but a quota of people in life
Who procure the happiness and the strife;
There are innumerable people with different traits,
Each with their individual loves and hates.

But why the existence of humankind,
Leaves me baffled and vexes my mind.

SONNET TO INCONGRUITY

Mankind has progressed from caves to technology,
Yet has regressed from love to animosity;
Humankind can be benevolently disposed,
But they are all too ready to kill their foes.

Some people are malicious, obnoxious and facetious,
While others are benignant, considerate and veracious.

Thus the balance is maintained on earth,
But what in Heaven is it all worth?
Everything revolves round money, it appears,
Living for Mammon for all of their years;
Some people allow it to dominate their lives,
Collecting it like nectar, as bees in their hives.

And for what, since when we die it stays behind,
As we enter a vacuum that's undefined.

SONNET TO INVESTMENT

The whole idea of life seems convoluted,
For serious ideals have been substituted
By mundane idols like financial reward
Where all depends upon what we can afford.

Surely man's existence has more relevance than this –
If not, then it's a life I would prefer to miss;
For money does not rate at all on my list –
Only one love induces me to exist.

A love which is implacable and perspicacious,
Constant, insouciant and pertinacious;
A love which to my heart is palatable and true;
A love which to my soul is immutable all through.

A coherent, real love that's beyond compare;
But being unrequited, there's no one to share.

SONNET TO IMPASSIVITY

Emotions make humans strong, but also weak,
Depending on the kind you're susceptible to.
Feelings within you can make you proud or meek –
They can also produce joy as well as rue.

Emotions dominate our every move,
Although often they have to be repressed.
Emotions cause us to praise or reprove
And for this life provide our inner zest.

Regularly I wish I could cast them aside
And be indifferent and devoid of feeling,
Never to give in to hate, jealousy and pride –
Neither to love or shame would I be yielding.

Languor and panic would have no place in my life;
I would be insensitive to happiness and to strife.

SONNET TO CLARITY

Sometimes I feel peevish and insecure
And remorseful, acrid and tantalised;
On other occasions I'm presumptuous and sure,
Probably because my life's disorganised.

Sometimes I feel aggrieved and acerbated
By all the fallaciousness I perceive,
And all this Jesus has expiated –
Yet still this life continues to deceive.

And although by Creation I am bemused,
I shall not dissipate my life for I love
A lady by whom I am not confused,
For she's prettier than all the angels above.

My love for her in my heart doth promote
An ardour my soul will never demote.

SONNET TO DEVOTION

Linda, your inordinate loveliness is beyond compare,
Your visage has a pulchritude that's radiant and bright;
Your countenance holds a comeliness that's unique and fair
And I am indebted to God for the gift of sight.

'For love comes by looking,' a philosopher once said,
And when I beheld your person my love for you was born;
And each day with thoughts of you my love is fed,
And it's a love that from my heart will never be torn.

Love is defined as caring for another more than oneself,
And my prayers for your well-being dominate my soul;
While thoughts of self-concern stay on the lowest shelf,
For this superlative love provides my earthly role.

So forever, Linda, you I will always revere
Because you're so talented, beautiful and sincere.

SONNET TO AMBITION

If I felt inclined, I could endeavour to write
A book solely for financial gain,
About an impavid agent who relished a fight
Or of a man whose lust he could not contain.

But I would not engage my time on such fiction,
As my inward policy is to only screeve
My true thoughts and not any contradiction
And all I consider I genuinely believe.

Even aspirations of what I would like to be –
And as with everything there is a reason for these –
For my hopes and desires make me glad I'm free,
But really I'm not allowed to do all that I please.

For I would like to chase after constant success;
But while life is mediocre, like most I care less.

SONNET TO PERFIDY

Emotions make humans formidable indeed –
History proves this beyond any reason;
In the last world war the Allies did succeed
In defeating those who committed worldwide treason.

People were destroyed as ants in their nest,
Annihilated and maimed beyond recognition,
Until their threat had been finally suppressed,
And now we all mourn these acts of attrition.

It's no good people being lugubrious of war
While attempting to precipitate an earthly peace,
For surreptitiously they scheme behind a closed door
Deciding which country should next lose its lease.

The hypocrisy and conflictions leave people nonplussed
And improvident to see within whose power they're trussed.

SONNET TO REVELATION

Everyone believes in their own cosmogony,
Although to others it appears inscrutable;
Even to oneself it can be dark as ebony
Or as bright as the sun, which is immutable.

But how do we associate what we do not know
About God and the afterworld, Heaven and Hell,
With all that goes on down here below
In this equivocal world where we buy and sell?

It agitates me at not knowing why
There is all this earthly ambiguity –
Always the truth and yet many a lie,
And the earth revolves on in continuity.

I hanker to have this enigmatic problem solved,
But only in my death will it truly be resolved.

SONNET TO HYPOCRISY

Some people are born into families poor;
Others are born into ones of wealth.
Some of those lacking money at this feel sore
And are spurred on to find riches with guile and stealth.

And when they do, what more do they gain?
Fame in this life and a larger stone for their grave.
And those who are rich look on with disdain
Upon those who like misers subsist and save.

Although I abjure money as a virulent idol,
It's a necessary means for one's existence;
But for some people it's an obsession they can't bridle
And to it they abnegate with no resistance.

And the supposedly judicious Royal Family of sybarites
Hypocritically accuse some folk of being parasites.

SONNET TO DILIGENCE

I respect anyone who builds a mountain from nought,
And sometimes them I wish I could emulate;
For success by their sheer determination is wrought
With resolute feelings which their minds inundate.

But some people try, yet are rejected
And relegated to being only second best;
Believe me, I know what it's like to be dejected
In this life where all we do seems to be a test.

Competition over harmony appears to prevail –
No wonder enmity in this world is rife,
Where people are prepared others to assail
Because a hostile action feels like a knife.

Offended dignity makes tempers flare
And then people act devoid of care.

SONNET TO RELIGION

Many religions in this world we find
And one is entitled to have one's own;
And in doing, be belligerent or kind,
Until we terminate this earthly loan.

But whether one's God be above or beneath,
One follows adheringly to His law;
And when one goes, remembrance comes in a wreath
And our life and beliefs will matter no more.

Each person has a religion to suit his mind's prism –
It could be Catholicism, Zionism or being a Quaker,
A Protestant, an atheist or in Lutherism,
Or even in football, oneself or being a moneymaker.

Ideally to the world these religions should be benignant,
Yet Northern Ireland and the Middle East proved them malignant.

SONNET TO JUBILANCE

If one wakes feeling salubrious and gay
It's a reason to be entirely glad;
For illness always makes one truly sad,
Depressed and lamentful of a wasted day.

So in this life where many complain
About adverse weather, the time flying by,
Insufficient money or people who lie,
It's best to once in a while refrain.

And from cursing what's scurrilous to abstain,
But instead breathe a contented sigh
At being fit and well and wholly sane
And ignore the turpitude that draws nigh,
And admire what virtues there do remain –
Achieve this, then you'll be on a high.

SONNET TO BEWILDERMENT

No two people are exactly the same
In this short life here on earth,
Throughout the time from one's birth
Until death does make its claim.

We're all different, each with a name,
Some with advantages over the rest –
But they do not always use them best,
And for all this injustice who's to blame?

To allow it, mankind has cause for shame,
For treating people as in a game.
But one has a right to pursue one's aim,
Whether it is for money, love or fame.
Yet this life is transient as a flame
And I'm bedevilled as to why here I came.

SONNET TO INEPTITUDE

There are times when I yearn
To be someone respected,
Instead of being subjected
To failing in my turn.

But from mistakes I try to learn
And see how life's connected,
For all success is reflected
By what you build, not burn.

Predestined, life appears to be
As with us all it does unfold;
But what would take delight with me
Would be for mine to be retold.
Winners or losers, although we're free,
We can't be choosers, for our life's controlled.

SONNET TO INADEQUACY

No matter whatever the situation,
Seldom do I use the proper phrase –
But the wrong one as if in a daze
And not having had prior contemplation.

Actions, whether in work or recreation,
Are the same as though I'm in a haze
And unable to escape from the maze
Of doing or desisting at each confrontation.

Always after the incident is past
I realise what I should have done or said;
If only I was capable of thinking fast
And acting correctly straight from my head.
But no, only after does logic come at last.
Thus being deficient, I will stay in bed.

SONNET TO EMINENCE

Linda, the reason I compose this verse
Is to honour your distinction.
Although it may seem somewhat terse,
It still conveys my instinction.

So versatile in dramatic art,
Your acting talent has no equal;
This praise for you comes from the heart
And to your skill it is a sequel.

Aussi de mon coeur does flow
A constant, ardent love for you;
With it my heart and mind do glow
And, no matter what, will see me through.

Of all the things I've been gleaning,
Only this love has any meaning.

SONNET TO CATHEXIS

On one calm September day
Was born a lovely female cat.
She was tortoiseshell, sleek and gay
As I watched her play on the mat.

Within a month she was in our home,
And was soon familiar with the place;
Then outside she was allowed to roam,
And everywhere in the garden she'd race.

She was responsive, clever and so sprightly
And attractive with her snow-white paws;
Tiptoes was her name and quite rightly,
For with them she could open doors.

Her big green eyes matched her colourful fur,
And always when stroked she'd pleasantly purr.

SONNET TO DESOLATION

Tiptoes, or more often Mamute or Fluff,
As by these names she was known,
Was always gentle and infrequently rough
Even when she became fully grown.

Many a time by her stealth were caught
Dozens of birds and the occasional mouse.
Always to us happiness she brought,
But it ended soon after changing house.

She seemed to settle at our home in the village,
But later she lay dead in a nearby estate,
The people of which as revenge I could pillage;
But it's still a mystery how her life did abate.

I am extremely vexed at not knowing why
Our four-year-old feline had to die.

SONNET TO INFATUATION

Linda, your peerless beauty
Is truly without flaw;
I will it to be my duty
To love you for evermore.

This love does me succour,
For it is all I do ensconce:
This love for you, *mon amour*,
Is a true innate response.

Fate keeps us apart, it seems,
But I will not be satisfied
Until I can fulfil my dreams
And be near you, by your side.

Although this I deeply desire,
I am only able to aspire. . . .

SONNET TO TELEOLOGY

Life is a tangible transient trek through time,
Seemingly controlled by our own actions;
Yet to another's orders we appear to mime –
That person being the God of all factions.

But why does He not make Himself apparent
So we can understand this earthly mystery?
Irresolute I am while He is transparent,
Irrespective of the events in history.

I sense God exists, but why the Creation?
Does He want us to emulate Jesus the Saviour?
Between humans and God what is the relation?
Could it be that He wishes to test our behaviour?

Surely if only goodness He would like us to pursue,
He has the power to inculcate us with His virtue.

SONNET TO APTITUDE

Titania, divine queen of Shakespeare's play,
This part you did enact with wonderful zeal.
As 'Avenger' Tara King for a while you did stay –
Your deftness is recorded on many a reel.

Nothing surpasses the happiness brought
When I was able to meet you vis-à-vis;
Always by me your company is sought,
For you I yearn to see frequently.

If I was able to win your admiration,
Then much more nearly would our lives revolve.
The fact we are not in the same constellation
Is an attempt to make my hope dissolve.

My love for you, Linda, is warmly intense;
It is genuine, honest and void of pretence.

SONNET TO INCONSISTENCY

Life is a period we live out
Like a diary written in advance;
Nothing is left to luck or chance –
Of this in my mind there is no doubt.

The only two times God has any say
Are when you are conceived in the womb
And when you are required in your tomb
Ready for the impending Judgement Day.

Some people, it seems, are already judged,
For they are born into the world lame;
People simply say, "Oh, what a shame,"
But why should they have fairness begrudged?

So if you are not born deformed or blind,
Give gratitude to God for being so kind.

SONNET OF ACCLAIM

Her real appellation is Marie,
Although Lulu is her stage name;
It was back in 1963
That with The Luvvers she gained fame.

Her immense beauty and dulcet voice,
Her natural appeal and mien so bland,
Make her as a singer my foremost choice
And with her real talent she needs no band.

My emotions by her mellifluous voice are roused,
With such songs as 'To Sir, with Love' and 'Let's Pretend'.
My admiration for her will never be doused,
For she assuages me while with this world I contend.

Vivacity and complaisance Lulu has inborn,
And her singing is more captivating than the dawn.

SONNET TO INCOMPATIBILITY

No matter whatever your profession,
It's always a case of 'us' and 'them';
For 'us' there must be a concession,
While 'them' we are supposed to condemn.

Unity is sought by the world's leaders,
But their efforts are hopelessly in vain;
A solution evades the most learned readers,
And so it will be till the end of man's reign.

So many people fail to comprehend
That equity cannot ever preside,
Until they eventually condescend
And rid themselves of emotions like pride.

Goodness, admittedly, many thousands has freed,
But it's pointless until we can extirpate greed.

SONNET TO DISCONSOLATION

I was calm, cool and collected,
But anxious for the final to begin;
As I walked on to the court I reflected
That I was extremely eager to win.

The tennis balls bounced to and fro
As there we warmed up on the Centre Court;
Then the umpire announced the word 'go',
And I began to play as I had been taught.

At two sets all we were evenly matched:
7–5, 5–7, 4–6, 6–4.
Then, by breaking my serve, the lead he snatched.
And the fifth set ended with 6–8 as the score.

I acted as though it had not mattered,
But really my dream he had just shattered.

SONNET TO DESPAIR

Many aspects of this life bring me down,
Caused mainly by men of this human breed.
The debased state of the world makes me frown,
All because God's commands mankind didn't heed.

Many loathsome men abuse their counterparts.
They disparage and with money entice young girls,
And under pretence of love con women's hearts
And exploit them in exchange for fame and pearls.

People are disparate as flakes of snow,
Hence the flagrant turmoil that comes to pass.
Similar in form, but unequal we grow,
Each given pastures of a different grass.

People only do what they believe they must,
But what they do, others don't conceive as just.

SONNET TO CAPRICE

The rain pounded on the windowpane
Like a deafening drum roll from a band;
Droplets of rain came through the cracked frame –
I brushed them aside swiftly with my hand.

All day it had rained without respite;
The sullen sky made me sombrely sigh.
Suddenly it stopped and the sun shone bright,
Revealing the forecast to be a lie.

Short-lived this remission turned out to be,
For very soon it was pouring down once more.
The clouds were a blindfold – the sun couldn't see,
As the atmosphere decreed its own law.

There's a likeness between myself and the erratic weather:
I also am changeable and to my own laws I tether.

SONNET TO LASCIVIOUSNESS

Sex is an urge, love is a desire;
Sex is but an animal crave.
Love is a feeling much more higher,
And to the latter I am a willing slave.

Sex for its own sake I do detest;
Its real purpose is man's continuity.
Some people with money readily invest
To produce abominable promiscuity.

Sexual permissiveness does abound
As a release from strict Victorian times;
Greater satisfaction they've supposedly found
With morbid abortions amongst their crimes.

An act designed for nuptial consummation
Is debased to a form of loose recreation.

SONNET TO CUPIDITY

Money dictates one's terrestrial abode;
Money dictates the way one will dress;
Money dictates one's transport for the road;
Money dictates one's rate of success.

Money dictates one's class of friend;
Money dictates the food one will eat;
Money dictates whether you borrow or lend;
Money dictates what orders you mete.

Money dictates how one passes the hours;
Money dictates over what one can buy;
Money dictates the extent of one's powers;
It may even govern when one will die.

Deplorable money does not rule what I cherish;
Money is ephemeral, but my loves will not perish.

SONNET TO CONSTERNATION

Constant criticism conduces cynicism;
Commendation cajoles our civility.
Curiosity creates our catechism;
Cephalic commands control our ability.

Communication merely does confound
And causes contradiction and confliction.
Conventions should our crises compound,
But they never contract a curing conviction.

Citizens convoke in a chanting concourse
To combat, canvass and campaign for changes,
While curators constrain them within contours,
Neither in concord or cognisant of dangers.

God conceived it condign that humans should have speech,
Yet competition and corruption are all that we teach.

SONNET TO PERCEPTION

With this world I cannot come to terms,
Mainly because of all the fallacies,
Affecting my senses like contagious germs
And perplexing my mind like parodies.

Altruism mankind must inculcate;
Virtuous acts we must concatenate.
It is sin that mankind does inculpate,
And it is this we must eradicate.

But man has adopted a complex guise
Living complacently without thinking;
Beyond his survival he has no eyes,
And about his future he has no inkling.

The irony is that man's pious conviction
Has turned to a dilemma of self-infliction.

SONNET TO DIVERSITY

It is incongruous to love and not know hate;
Inconsistent to not want and not know desire.
Hence people can be early and can be late,
And the same can also dislike and admire.

They can bestow invective as well as praise.
They can enjoy health or suffer illness,
Or work industriously or just laze,
And can be lively or prone to stillness.

Life is a display of truths and veneers –
A guessing game of refusal and selection.
We spend the many days contriving ideas
For subsequent acceptance or rejection.

The essence of life is to occupy time,
Just as I have done by composing this rhyme.

SONNET TO NOEL

Christmas to children means Santa Claus,
Gifts and novelties, crackers and cakes.
Professed Christians take time to pause,
For suddenly their faith reawakes.

They attend church as a social function,
Or as a duty to their posterity;
This yearly ritual stirs compunction,
And benevolence precedes their severity.

It is Christ's birth that some celebrate
With prayer, feasting and real charity;
Those who disbelieve, themselves inebriate,
And as a public holiday greet it with parity.

The Yule season promotes peace for a period brief,
Then mankind absurdly returns to his grief.

SONNET TO PROWESS

The leopard shrewdly crouched and froze
    And eyed its unsuspecting prey,
    Grazing peacefully yards away,
    Then once again the leopard arose.

The breeze blew into the cat's face
    As it crept nearer without sound
With stealthy precision along the ground,
Tensing its muscles for the coming chase.

Suddenly the leopard pounced with might
And the bewildered deer flinched with fright;
The cat raced forward like a beam of light
And a second too late the deer took flight.
The deer succumbed to the carnivore's right
    And was consumed in a tree that night.

SONNET TO MORALITY

God meant us to be civilised, not cannibals;
Yet still some humans act like animals,
Besmirching modesty with what is sordid
And to God's wishes they remain torpid.

'Marriage is honourable in all, and the bed undefiled'–
These are the words of God and not be to reviled.
'But whoremongers and adulterers God will judge',
So avoid salacity or your soul you smudge.

Jesus did say when us He redeemed,
That that which amongst men is esteemed
And causes earthly depredation
Would be His Father's deprecation.

Law-abiding people we should not infringe,
Nor upon their liberty should we impinge.

SONNET TO CHARITY

At Christmas time
Church bells chime
Pealing chords of joy;
There is no sin
For peace sets in
With every girl and boy.

A time to chant
And wishes grant
To all of human life;
Forget the bad,
Do not be sad –
Let merriment heal the strife.

While Christmas stays, it precludes pains
For several days, then it wanes. . . .

SONNET TO RESENTMENT

I dislike the word 'compulsion' –
It incites within revulsion;
I do believe ordinarily
In doing things voluntarily.

But this world says, "No –
You comply or go!"
So you do as you are told
Whether you are coy or bold.

This I do resent,
For I do not consent
To being snubbed or shoved –
That's why those not loved
Initiate their own revival
With violent acts of reprisal.

SONNET TO EXPOSITION

She portrayed Belinda in *The Provok'd Wife*,
A play about eighteenth-century life.
One scene called for a change of dress
Where she removed her bodice press;
Thus she displayed her gorgeous breasts and nipples –
Which through my spine sent sensuous ripples.

But I did not deem this right
That I should enjoy this sight;
So I turned my eyes aside
Until her nightie did preside,
So that each beautiful breast
Was now no longer divest.

This crass titillation may have added reality,
But degraded her thespian chasteness to banality.

SONNET TO RAMPAGE

The Federal soldiers fiercely charged
With rifles firing and pistols shooting.
Through barricaded doors they barged
And resorted to ravage and to looting.

They set buildings ablaze and watched them burn
And then set fire to the ripened corn.
For help, to whom could the Southerners turn?
And for their loss who would redress and mourn?

The marauders engaged in rape and plunder
And any Confederates were shot or repelled;
Their aggression was that of lightning and thunder
As they punished the people who had rebelled.

Saving the Confederacy now rested with Lee
As Sherman continued his march to the sea.

SONNET TO MODESTY

Here is a paradox of a kind:
Many people see, but are blind;
When they are imperilled from without,
It is to the aliens that they shout.
But then when threatened from within,
They readily rebuke their own kin.

Contradictory this may seem –
It is a truth and not a dream.
Just as I do not think it is rude
For a pretty woman to pose in the nude,
It only becomes perversely crude
When with prurient thoughts it is viewed.

Each person their own beliefs must find
Before they can achieve peace of mind.

SONNET TO RENEWAL

To people worldwide, what does Christmas mean?
Their ideas are as diverse as the sciences;
Yet one factor does make alliances
In that by all a festival it is seen.

In many a country and society,
It is a custom and tradition –
A time of gaiety and remission
Where routine defers to variety.

People pay homage to Christ's Nativity,
Then at Easter they tribute His ascension;
This will not banish all the iniquity
Until all of mankind has the intention.
But there's one event of no uncertainty –
Heralding the New Year with joyous convention.

SONNET OF TRIBUTE

Your melodious voice does me soothe
And fills my heart with warm elation;
Hearing you sing expels all my rues
And pacifies the storm of creation.

The storm that rages all around,
Blowing away the jigsaw pieces,
So the solution won't be found
Until the adverse weather ceases.

But while my mind with your song is replete,
Astuteness replaces my temerity;
And no longer do I feel I'm effete,
For strength circulates with celerity.

Marie, you instil tranquillity of mind,
And parts of life's puzzle you help me to find.

SONNET TO RESTITUTION

My idea of what could be paradise
Would be to live on a luscious isle,
Sufficiently big to take exercise
And far away from the world so vile.

Away from the struggles of pride and hate,
Away from the falsity and the vanity,
I would live according to nature's fate
With the lady I love to keep my sanity.

A situation of similar exactness
Was instigated through Adam and Eve;
But their gross disobedience was tactless
And God decided that they should leave.

The death we all endure is God's reproach
Because His sovereignty they did encroach.

SONNET TO COMMUNION

Almighty God, I thank You dearly
For allowing me this sacrament;
Enable me to see more clearly
What in this life is pertinent.

I beseech You, Lord, enrich my mind
And in my acts let goodness flourish,
So that with Your grace I might find
Such love on which my soul may nourish.

Please keep me on Your beaten track
As I stumble through this life;
Let not my faith show any crack
In confronting any strife.

Finally I implore that those oppressed
Will turn to You and in Your love invest.

SONNET TO IDIOM

Pipe dreams, pie in the sky,
Keeping up with the Jones,
Irons in the fire, fish to fry,
Breaking even, sticks and stones . . .

Bureaucracy and red tape,
Toiling to bring home the bacon,
Blowing out or getting in shape,
Sounding off, no offence taken . . .

Falling by the wayside, losing out,
Sitting pretty, coming up trumps,
Pulling together, in with a shout,
Fuelling the blaze, smoothing the bumps . . .

Having to say something, then clichés we use,
But with something to say our words become news.

SONNET TO EXPRESSION

A fool and his money are soon parted,
But how did the fool achieve his worth?
Dying for God will get you martyred,
Yet who wants to inherit the earth?

A rolling stone gathers no moss
Unless you're put in a stagnant pond.
One man's gain is another man's loss,
Except when you win with a Premium Bond.

If music be the food of love, then
Listening to Rod Stewart will give you colic!
If at first you don't succeed, try again –
No, drown your woe with a gin and tonic!

Such sayings are statements after the fact
To excuse the providence that we lacked.

SONNET TO MODERNITY

What do we need to survive in life?
Food in our bellies, shoes on our feet;
Yet the world is endemic with strife
And haggling over the price of wheat.

What else do we require to exist?
Clothes on our back, water to drink;
Yet Westerners compile a shopping list
That won't, until death, finally shrink.

What more can assist our well-being?
Shelter from the cold, a shoulder to lean on.
Our selfishness leaves sights unseen –
The suffering of others we're not keen on.

Getting enough is our compulsive concern;
But to people with less, we have money to burn.

SONNET TO PAP

Rushed off one's feet
Or having time to kill,
There's no way to cheat
Life's one bitter pill.

So make hay while the sun shines;
Strike when the iron is hot,
For under the earth's confines
It's forever that we rot.

While happiness is our pursuit,
There's many a slip 'twixt cup and lip;
So tread lightly with hobnailed boot –
Give others a fair crack of the whip.

Not knowing what's around the bend,
Don't ask for chips you cannot spend.

SONNET TO CHIVALRY

Playing against somebody at squash
Is like medieval jousting;
Losing is like being under the cosh
Or suffering an ignoble ousting.

In comparison, winning's a relief,
Whereby you emerge blithely unscathed,
And then claim the fair maiden's handkerchief,
While your armorial standard is raised.

With squash it is a similar story
When you force your opponent to yield,
Then as victor you bask in the glory
As the vanquished trudges from the field.

Triumph preserves honour and nurtures your pride,
But defeat is a worm that gnaws you inside.

SONNET TO LINDA

Linda, I've loved you all the while,
For unremitting is my zeal;
But I've been tainted by life's dour bile
And cannot find an even keel.

Indefeasible, like fairy tales,
My feelings are inconsequential;
For though they are the wind in my sails,
They are lashed by rain that's torrential.

But metaphors and similes aside,
My disenchantment grows;
For platitudes cannot hide
The maelstrom my mind knows.

My life irredeemable, my love unrequited,
What is there remaining? What is there not blighted?

SONNET TO AFTERS

Cherry cheesecake
Close to the lake,
Then chased down with Earl Grey tea.

Black Forest gateau
Will make her face glow
While we nibble on some Brie.

Hot treacle tart
Should warm her heart
As she nestles next to me.

Lemon meringue,
Its tingling tang,
For her love might be the key.

Victoria sponge –
What is this gunge!

SONNET TO SECONDS

Crisp crêpes Suzette
After we had met
Suggested she might play.

Jam roly-poly
Eaten very slowly
As beside her I lay.

Spotted dick and custard –
She knew for her I lusted
And could not keep away.

Raisin and apple strudel,
Then I begged like a poodle
That she would make my day.

Blancmange and rum baba –
Thanks for the sweets – ta-ta!

SONNET TO SYNERGISM

Do you love me?
Do I love you?
Now do you see
My point of view?

If I can give,
Then you will take,
So you may live
Just for my sake.

It matters not
That you might think
There's not a lot
Beyond a drink.

The moment's fine:
I'm yours, you're mine.

SONNET TO CONUNDRUM

I confess to a propensity
For revering beautiful girls,
So discover the identity
Of this maiden with skin like pearls.

The first letter would be her cup size;
Her second is most in evidence;
The next two merit the booby prize;
The fifth is me in another sense.

End her forename with singular 'ease'
And start her surname by yelling, "Hey!"
The second sounds like a 'z' in tease;
The third is rife in 'hip hip hooray'.

The final two will come by and by,
Then in her midst you'll be on a high.

SONNET TO INFERIORITY

Losing – there is nothing worse.
Being second best, an also ran,
Coming second, is a curse –
The wretched never-never man.

But then winning takes some nerve.
Playing safe will not suffice;
You must assert yourself with verve
As if throwing with loaded dice.

Participation is fine –
If you can stomach defeat.
But that's where I draw the line;
Humble pie I loathe to eat.

While my flair is in short supply,
Nobody can say I don't try.

SONNET TO ASSIMILATION

Understanding is the predicate by which
We formulate opinions of the world;
That life is an uneven playing pitch
Is one that's regularly unfurled.

Our ideas of fair play are coloured
By how we see that others are treated;
We can condone a person being mullered
If it is justice that's being meted.

Acceptable behaviour is what is expected –
A game of empirical extrapolation,
So our actions become interconnected
In response to media dissemination.

We are all chameleons trying to cope,
Adapting, changing and living in hope.

SONNET TO PROJECTION

Squash is a sport of hit and retrieve,
A racket game of attack and defend.
It involves exertion without reprieve,
And for the best of five one does contend.

A game of stamina coupled with skill,
It's imperative to gain control of the 'T';
From there a short ball one's able to 'kill',
And thereby dominate the rallies to be.

For some, the game discharges aggression;
To others it's just vigorous exercise.
For me, it is a palliative obsession,
And others merely do it to fraternise.

Gregarious I'm not, indefatigable I am,
Persevering for success and devoid of all sham.

SONNET TO INAUTHENTICITY

The seriousness of life
Does lend itself to meaning,
With reasons that are rife
To prop our every leaning.

So actions that seem bona fide
Are all laced with subterfuge,
Until behind it we all hide
And the human lie grows huge.

Thus we all know where we're at,
And our motives seem to hold true;
But our ideas soon fall flat
When we question the things we do.

If as adults we could be born,
Of our pretension we'd be shorn.

SONNET TO EMOTIVISM

So what is disgust?
Just what does it mean?
Wherein is its thrust
From which we can glean?

Does it mean disapproval
Or merely dismay?
Does it dictate removal
From the field of play?

Does it impute wrong-doing
Or only distaste?
Perhaps it's self-viewing
Presuming what's chaste.

More likely it's a watershed,
A distillation in one's head.

SONNET TO MUHAMMAD ALI

Charles 'Sonny' Liston
Fought like a piston,
But you fouled up his works.

You changed your name,
Wouldn't play their game,
So they took away your perks.

Then George Foreman you tamed
And the title reclaimed
To show your skills were not quirks.

With opponents outclassed
And records surpassed,
You've proven that boxers aren't jerks.

The ideals that you taught, the respect that you brought,
Your nobility of thought – in your awe we're caught.

SONNET TO QUANDARY

The simple truth is that nothing matters;
But if we accept this, ourselves we deny,
Leaving life's meaning in complete tatters
By dashing beliefs on which we rely.

Things are important when we care,
For then we listen and love and learn;
When we don't, it's as if they're not there,
Like kindling needs oxygen to burn.

That we're significant with innate worth
Is the assumption we've come to espouse.
That way there's reason for treading this earth
And not living inanely as a mouse.

So now we know that life's premise is sound,
Only death's purpose has need to be found.

SONNET TO STRICTURE

So much time on our hands,
But we have one-night stands.

So much food from which to choose,
Yet it's weight we want to lose.

So many places to visit,
But we think television exquisite.

So many tipples to imbibe,
Yet their contents we can't describe.

Innumerable people to meet,
But the mere thought gives us cold feet.

An infinity of things to learn,
Yet the opportunity we spurn.

The excesses we have supersede
The sole essence of life, which is need.

SONNET TO VAPIDITY

At the end of the day you look back
And consider what you have done;
Of mundane matters you will lose track
While you'll remember what was fun.

Life can seem incredibly dull,
Unless punctuated with thrills;
Thus we contrive to pierce the lull
Of just working to pay the bills.

So we devise a web of distraction
To camouflage our basic whims
With events for our own satisfaction,
Then purge our conscience singing hymns.

Excoriate our sententious pursuits
And you're left with uninteresting roots.

SONNET TO ATTITUDE

Does it matter to you
What I do?
If you're polite,
Then it might.

Other than that
It's tit for tat,
Or mutual action
Based on attraction.

So we intermix
To find a fix,
To beat the blues,
To search for clues.

But above all of these,
It is social disease.

SONNET TO APPETENCE

What is it about Maria
Whenever I chance to see her?

She is always good news –
Her being ignites my fuse.

She's much tastier than sangria,
More ravishing than Boadicea.

Like garnets her eyes sparkle,
And she has more curves than Arkle.

Even in papier-mâché collars
She would look a million dollars.

If she ran in the Derby I'd back her,
And I'd pull her if she was a cracker.

But the reason I'm beset is simple:
It is her dainty, disarming dimple.

SONNET TO ALIGNMENT

Relationships don't have rules –
They function simply on trust.
That's why we are often fools
In mistaking love for lust.

For those we know, we wear
Our heart on our jacket sleeve;
For others, we do not care
If our words are make-believe.

Understanding what we're about
Is the crux of our being alive;
Knowing when to whisper or shout
Decides whether we wilt or thrive.

The dreams of many are enacted by few,
But reality for all is in making do.

SONNET TO ADVERSITY

If you're feeling down,
Then do not frown –
Just play the clown.

If things are rough,
Do not get tough –
Resort to bluff.

If you're on the brink,
Don't turn to drink –
Stop and think.

If you're off the track,
Do not go back –
Change your tack.

If life seems bad, don't curse,
For that could make it worse.

SONNET TO CLAPTRAP

What does it matter?
Does anyone care?
It's just idle chatter –
Neither here nor there.

So why do we natter?
To comment and compare;
Just pointless patter
About who, when and where.

Like the noisy clatter
Of breaking chinaware,
People merely spatter,
"I've nothing to declare."

We effuse cheek to cheek,
But it's all doublespeak.

SONNET TO PERSONALITY

Can you mimic Tommy Cooper?
Are you a collector of stamps?
Do you subscribe to BUPA?
Have you seen Susan George at Tramps?

Can you cook chilli con carne?
Are you a UFO believer?
Do you think *Neighbours* is barmy?
Have you got a golden retriever?

Can you play the balalaika?
Are you able to spell 'doolally'?
Do you holiday in Jamaica?
Have you been to a Greenpeace rally?

If so you'll have friends by the score;
If not you'll be snubbed as a bore.

SONNET TO PAWKINESS

Freddie Mercury is gone,
So Queen no longer reigns;
Let us hold a telethon
To help his mate from Staines.

Frankie Howerd no longer pisses,
Having made his final titter,
So his catchphrase 'Ooh, no, missus'
Will now need a babysitter.

Benny Hill's sell-by date is past –
No longer will he leer;
And all feminists, scrawny-arsed,
No doubt will give a cheer.

So ashes to ashes and dust to dust,
Carry on ogling Barbara Windsor's bust!

SONNET TO CONTEMPT

Dropping litter,
Snorting cocaine,
Being a quitter,
Smashing porcelain.

Jumping queues,
Evading one's fare,
Scratching church pews,
Driving without care.

Never saying please,
Not flushing the loo,
An unshielded sneeze,
Blocking someone's view.

Picking one's nose –
Anything goes!

SONNET TO OPTIMUM

Happiness is getting up
Without any aches or pains;
Happiness is a growing pup
That we walk along the lanes.

Happiness is a Cadbury's Flake
Melting slowly on your tongue;
Happiness for its own sake,
Like a Frisbee that is flung.

Happiness is a cancerous spot
That turns out to be a mole;
Happiness is being in the Kop
When Liverpool score a goal.

Happiness exists in the mind
Where each of us has it defined.

SONNET TO APATHY

Nothing much to report
In my boring life of rote;
Maybe I've been sold short,
Or simply just missed the boat.

It's all inconsequential,
So tediously drab,
And truly non-essential
Like an anti-bliss jab.

It appears all the same to me –
One day rolls into the next;
Yet my gaoler I cannot see,
And I can't amend the text.

But why languish in such sorrow?
The answer will come tomorrow. . . .

SONNET TO SCHMALTZ

Happiness is bright, sunny weather,
Or finding the last train seat;
Happiness is a coming-together,
Or a holiday in Crete.

Happiness is learning with no revision,
Or the last digestive in the tin;
Happiness is making the right decision,
Or shaving without nicking your chin.

Happiness is listening to Beach Boys hits,
Or with a girl's beauty being smitten;
Happiness is a slap-up meal at the Ritz,
Or playing with a fluffy kitten.

Happiness is an apple you bite and savour,
Briefly, then all you have left is the flavour.

SONNET TO INITIATION

Now I'm here, first things first –
My craving for Mother's milk;
Sate my hunger, quench my thirst,
Then I'll discover my ilk.

After it's schooling and learning letters,
Finding my place in the pecking order,
Identifying who are my betters
And that conformity is life's warder.

Then I'm expected to earn a crust
And conduct myself in a sensible manner,
Never forgetting in God we trust
Even though it was man who forged the spanner.

Having been taught what life entails,
There's no reason for leaving the rails.

SONNET TO SAVOUR

Happiness is just a state of mind,
The feeling of being contented;
It is respite from the daily grind,
Or having your life augmented.

More often than not it's fleeting
Like a bright rainbow after the storm;
It could be an impromptu meeting,
A kind remark that isn't the norm.

Frequently it's an achievement
That translates into a smile;
Conversely a sudden bereavement
Is liable to disgorge bile.

Ecstasy for some is found in a pill;
Others are satisfied with a cheap thrill!

SONNET TO DENIER

Our frailty at birth is seen,
But with age is soon forgotten;
On immortality we wean,
Though our lives are threads of cotton:

Easily torn and eventually frayed,
The material of life is tenuous;
Whether it be chiffon or worsted plaid,
The shirt-pulling can be strenuous.

The teguments we sport through the years
Lend credence to our worldly standing;
Yet while a parachute allays fears,
It does not ensure a soft landing.

Thus a Savile Row suit may open doors,
But death will finally level the scores.

SONNET TO ADOLESCENCE

In recalling my youth,
I remember being fazed –
The duplicity of truth
Left me fuddled and glazed:

Shirley Bassey in décolletage robes
Moved slinkily on the TV screen,
And I'd be fascinated by her globes
As they bulged underneath the sateen.

Thus my arousal unfolded
With my sodden pubescence,
But by my church priest was scolded
For such sinful excrescence.

So did this spiritual and carnal clash
Cause my acne – that accursed rash!

SONNET TO ENDEAVOUR

To Milton Keynes I came,
In the marathon to compete;
Finally left in shame,
As the time limit I didn't beat.

Four hours seventeen minutes twelve seconds
It took me to finish the race:
Hardly a time that for a medal beckons,
Unless I'd gone out at walking pace!

Still, I completed the course,
Even though my lungs were aching;
The next day I was a bit hoarse
And my legs were a long time waking.

Despite the discomfort and displeasure,
At least I discovered my true measure.

SONNET TO BREAKDOWN

(Fault-finding – '62-stock Tube train)

"You're going along", Albert said,
"When you sense something is wrong.
The power control is dead –
So coast if it isn't too long.

"When you stop and secure, check traction,
Then train line and main-line air;
Trip and reset and try for action –
If nothing happens, don't despair.

"Next in sequence, give it one back,
Reverse your control guv'nor if it goes;
If not, don't have a heart attack –
Change the twenty-amp fuse and see if it blows.

"If movement is obtained, be happy;
Otherwise sit tight and change your nappy!"

Footnote: This sonnet relates to the workings of the Central Line Tube stock on the London Underground.

SONNET AD NAUSEAM

Is anybody really concerned
About the Iraqi arms scandal?
Does it matter what Lord King earned
Or if soccer's Vinnie Jones is a vandal?

Is it pertinent that Charles and Di
Faced an irreconcilable rift?
And who cares whether it's a lie
That Mellor was suborned with a 'gift'?

So what if women priests may cause a schism,
Or Lloyds' members face exorbitant claims,
Or the pound leaves the Exchange Rate Mechanism,
Or Windsor Castle is consumed by flames?

What's relevant about closures of pits?
It's all beginning to get on my . . . wits!

SONNET TO FRIPPERY

The minimum depth of one metre
Is needed for a water-polo game.
Steve Cauthen can be a world-beater –
The Kentucky Kid is his nickname.

Curling, netball and water polo
Have seven people on each side;
An 'abundance' is found in solo,
While a goal is eight yards wide.

Tommy Docherty was quoted as saying,
"Jack Nicklaus hasn't had more clubs than me."
There are twenty-eight dominoes when playing,
While a drop goal in rugby league scores three.

Mark Spitz accumulated nine medals all told;
'87 saw Fatima win our sole gold.

SONNET TO DESSERT

Apple crumble
And a frisky fumble
With Deborah in a rick.

Peaches and cream
Down by the stream
Where I ask her for a lick.

Raspberry ripple
With hock to tipple
Will probably do the trick.

Ice-cream sundae
And some foreplay –
I believe I'm feeling sick!

Chocolate mousse –
Oh, what's the use!

SONNET TO RESURGENCE

Making up the numbers –
That seems to be my role;
And like a dog that slumbers,
I wouldn't bother a soul.

Yet as the match progressed,
I floundered but did not fret.
Then came my rival's bequest:
A game that my thirst did whet.

With a chance to upset the form,
I galvanised myself to compete;
And after weathering the storm,
My antagonist tasted defeat.

'Who dares wins' is usually fudge,
But even a Parker pen will smudge.

SONNET TO CONJUGATION

Alan and Sara: two fine people
That Destiny has thrown together,
And married beneath a church steeple
To become birds of one feather.

For them we hope the future bodes well
With pleasant occasions to savour;
Having tied the knot their love will gel
With no cause to fall out of favour.

We pray they'll be bathed in success
With good fortune to towel them down,
And if nothing they'll always possess
A love that will dispel any frown.

So here we toast a perfect match –
Wish them good health and down the hatch.

SONNET TO RELEVANCE

If *The Prisoner* means anything to me,
Then it's because we have something to share:
A subliminal hankering to be free,
Overridden by a failure to dare.

In our longing to be recognised,
We overlook the attention we court,
Then gripe when crudely categorised
Because individuality is what's sought.

The Prisoner is surrealistically exact
About the numerical anonymity of being,
Where depersonalisation cannot detract
From the antithesis that conformity is freeing.

The imagery is transparently clear –
Singularity still needs others to cheer.

SONNET TO HUBRIS

Individually we exist, that's true,
But then so do blades of grass.
What's the difference between me and you?
Is it just a question of class?

That we're unique in isolation
Matters not to the sum of the whole;
What counts is interpretation
Of what we construe to be our role.

Independence may be what we seek,
But its innate value is up for grabs
Because scaling a tough mountain peak
Only has meaning when others keep tabs.

Thus what's worthwhile is just a con,
Since when you're dead the glory's gone.

SONNET TO ELABORATION

It was a random choice to pick number six,
Like forty-two for Adams explains it all.
The series' motif is you can't teach new tricks
To a headstrong old dog who ignores your call.

'Be seeing you' is but a harmless valediction;
The finger–thumb gesture is Masonic in kind.
The blazer with piping is just a depiction
That uniformity leads to an ordered mind.

'Rover' represents every person's worst fear;
Life's lottery is denoted with the numbers.
The penny farthing reminds us why we're here
And that progress unharnessed only encumbers.

The episodic need to extract information
Ends in an overload purged by conflagration.

SONNET OF ELUCIDATION

All manner of interpretation –
Syllogism, allegory, metaphor –
Can alleviate our consternation,
But still the rendition leaves us unsure.

Was Number Six his own worst enemy
In not conforming to the norm?
It's like expecting David Bellamy
To walk straight past an unknown corm.

The essential nature of the series
Revolves around one man's self-import;
The lesson being, which quells all queries,
Is that of not selling oneself short.

If your value has others concerned,
Ask yourself how such interest was earned.

SONNET TO EMPIRICISM

Lodestar, watershed, oracle and touchstone –
From these we develop our abstract ideals.
Through interpretation we start to hone
Our countless actions by which our life anneals.

Though our instinct to survive supersedes all,
Our behaviour is tempered by reflection;
For we determine whether we trip or fall
By curbing our caprice for predilection.

So having abjured what's considered nefarious,
We traipse the course of conformist sobriety,
Leaving our experience of evil vicarious
Fulfilled by media immune to propriety.

Thus chimerical notions escape objurgation,
But arrant deeds will attract moral condemnation.

SONNET TO FAMILIARITY

Role model,
Stereotype;
Chris Waddle,
Media hype.

TV dinner,
Unsafe sex;
Michael Winner,
Ray-Ban specs.

Mortgage arrears,
Right to vote;
Crocodile tears,
Learn by rote.

Scrambled eggs –
All life's pegs.

SONNET TO SOMEONE

To unveil this person, unravel this verse:
The first letter's like Hades, it is reckoned,
And first person singular is my second;
The third can be found in nostrum and nurse.

The next is commemorated every June,
The fifth is the impolite word for 'pardon'.
The sixth is present in set but not harden,
The seventh is aspirate, as in hewn.

The eighth is a figure owned by James Bond,
The ninth is one of three learnt at school.
The tenth letter's sibilant as in stool,
The penultimate's in rod but not in wand.

'Avenger' contains the final letter –
Now you should know this gorgeous go-getter.

SONNET TO CONSUMERISM

The hubble-bubble of advertising cant
Subjects our ears to subordinate tones:
"Buy this, buy that" is the anonymous rant.
"And we'll help you defray the costs with loans."

We're besought to buy commodities without restraint
And airy-fairy items like a personal fan;
To save time there's an undercoat and gloss in one paint
And a sunlamp that instantly gives you a tan.

We're encouraged to have products that are 'green',
So let's all ride bicycles and eat only grass!
The images portrayed on our TV screen
Say it matters which loo paper – what a farce!

In our humdrum lives we have egregious choices –
A humble existence or lavish Rolls-Royces.

SONNET TO AFFLATUS

Everything that needs to be explained
Can hardly be contained
In any encyclopaedia.

Any learning that's not ingrained
Can readily be obtained
By simply scanning the media.

Should it be instinct that is lacking
Let someone else do the attacking
To ensure that you survive.

If intuition is what you crave,
Then to others don't be a slave,
For innocence does not thrive.

Yet it's not understanding that contentment brings,
But establishing our place in the scheme of things.

SONNET TO LUBRICITY

Though her beauty is evanescent like a bloom,
Its effusion supplies my motor with 'vroom'.
Her dehiscent buds and Black Forest gateau
Are better proportioned than any chateau.

Without doubt her decor is avant-garde,
Her salient splendour completely unmarred.
But what's hard for me to come to grips
Is that I'll ne'er taste her treacly lips.

Her being serves only to evoke
Dreams wherein her bold breasts I stroke
And on their effluvium begin to choke;
Thereafter there is an empty chasm,
And I awaken with a fretful spasm
Never to know of her orgasm.

SONNET TO HOMOGENEITY

Life is entwined in tawdry red tape,
Each of us itemised, packaged and sent.
But to me it's all an elaborate jape
To suppress any innovative or artistic bent.

Having been date-stamped and properly labelled,
We're supposed to adopt our allotted roles;
But does it matter where a horse is stabled,
Unless you're interested in having foals?

Where duties prevail, decisions are negated,
And we're constrained to options, not personal selection.
Such conditioning, it can be remonstrated,
Is the price we pay for society's protection.

Our actions become based on an agglomeration
Of artificial premises of subordination.

SONNET TO REVEILLE

The alarm blares its staccato shrill,
Piercing my brain like a lance;
Should I arise, much against my will,
Or flop back in bed? – a fat chance!

Responsibility, duty, reliance and money –
Words that hammer on my mind's door;
Soggy cereals, burnt toast, glutinous eggs – not funny!
I'm impelled to yawn and sleep some more.

Inexorably the dilemma prickles compunction.
Surely freedom of thought means freedom of action;
So does lethargy constitute a valid malfunction
Or is it just sloth? – I'm driven to abstraction.

A minute has elapsed, now it's time to choose;
I loll over and press the button marked 'snooze'!

SONNET TO PENUMBRA

Asking if God lives is ostensibly insensate –
It's like enquiring about the consistency of air.
Or the existence of Cupid would you contemplate?
Only if he's presaging a sensuous love affair.

God has no pedigree, just the power to daunt,
Though His relevance to many is purely fugacious.
The desuetude of religion lends to the vaunt
That divine conciliation tends to be predacious.

God can be used to explain misfortune,
Or credited as life's orchestrator;
Others see Him as merely a rune –
An anthropomorphic procreator.

In this Stygian life we may find our place through God,
But does it mean like a horse we'll run better shod?

SONNET TO HELTER-SKELTER

While eating your Curly Wurly,
Lend a thought as to why you're here;
For amid life's hurly-burly
There are some with nothing to cheer.

You may call me a silly billy
For considering the lot of others,
Yet is fate acting willy-nilly
That one can say, "Fetch my Rolls, Caruthers"?

But nature's pyramid can be topsy-turvy
When subserviency breaks the mould;
For who will impugn the system as scurvy
If there's a chance to escape the fold?

To survive and succeed, don't shilly-shally –
Be decisive indeed and don't dilly-dally.

SONNET TO TRIVIA

In bridge, what does a yarborough hand lack?
Which sport has a Walrus, White Shark and Great Bear?
Boules has a *cochonnet*; what game has a jack?
Who danced the Bolero with majestic flair?

Which is the oldest English horse-race meeting?
Who competes for the MacRobertson shield?
Which boxer gave Ali a ten-round beating?
And how many play on a netball field?

In which game can the 'battery' be found?
And where would you see a dig, set and spike?
What sport can be seen at the Hickstead ground?
And which game uses a tolly to strike?

Football is 'kick-off'; what starts hockey on ice?
And, lastly, which team hosts at Tannadice?

Answers for 'Sonnet to Trivia'

A yarborough is a bridge hand that lacks any card higher than a nine.

Nicknames respectively, of golfers Craig Stadler, Greg Norman and Jack Nicklaus.

Bowls has a jack as the target ball.

Jayne Torvill and Christopher Dean skated spectacularly to the 'Bolero' in 1984.

The St Leger is the oldest English Classic horse-race meeting, established in 1776.

The MacRobertson Shield is a croquet trophy.

In his last fight, Ali was defeated by Canadian Trevor Berbick.

Netball is seven-a-side, so fourteen on the playing court.

'Battery' is a term used in American football.

You would 'dig, set and spike' in volleyball.

Hickstead showcases showjumping and hosts the International Horse of the Year event.

A 'tolly' is used in the game of marbles.

'Bully-off' begins a field hockey match ('face-off' is ice hockey).

Tannadice is the home of Scottish football team Dundee United.

SONNET TO DISABUSEMENT

Our activities are not far removed
From the harsh feral law of the jungle;
Such conduct is irrefutably proved
By the wars that form mankind's carbuncle.

But when we are safe, our acts mellow
And morals and ethics come to the fore;
"Love your enemies," some Christians bellow
Until belligerence raps upon their door.

People are not good, just well intentioned;
Nor are they bad, but merely maladjusted.
Thus convention rules when scruples are mentioned,
Yet in conflict with prejudice, cannot be trusted.

Each of us is no more than a drop in the ocean,
Making life a welter of superfluous commotion.

SONNET TO PARALLAX

With millions of pounds
I could resign my job;
I would pay off the hounds
And give the in-laws a few bob.

I'd buy a hotel in which to swank
(Insured with Norwich Union, of course).
The rest I'd invest in a good bank
And have the odd flutter on a horse.

Alternatively I'd book myself a cruise
Round the world on the grand *QE2* liner;
I'd buy a pad in some luxurious mews
And take squash coaching to make my game finer.

But the bulk I'd sink in a chateau in France
With luscious vineyards oozing white wine – fat chance!

SONNET TO RECALCITRANCE

I'm sick and tired of this corporeal mass
Not responding to my cogent will;
Time and again its actions are crass,
And when it's cold it catches a chill!

I tell it to write neatly, I ask it to sing,
I demand that it be aerobically fit;
Or would that it a pretty girl bring,
But no, it repels them by growing a zit!

So how am I supposed to exist
With my body estranged from volition?
It's like being dealt a chicane at whist
When a grand slam is my ambition.

The world's a stage and, though knowing my lines,
I'm a walk-on extra within fate's designs.

SONNET TO ANTITHESIS

While society's elite munch their pickled roe,
Greenpeace campaigns to save the whale;
And as the gamekeeper selects another doe,
The protest of vegans is to no avail.

While pesticides contaminate yet curtail disease,
Organic farmers proffer untainted wheat;
And to preclude our smelling like fetid cheese
We use aerosols which effect a 'glasshouse' heat.

While many a zoo CITES shortage of species,
Some vain people expropriate their pelts;
And for the glorious sake of winning VCs,
Nations explode bombs – so the ice cap melts.

Our conscience is the gimbal on which the world rests,
But thus far we've no reason for drumming our breasts.

SONNET TO IRRELEVANCE

In which film did Jim Carrey portray the Grinch?
Why is climbing a Munro an accomplished feat?
Is a capstan a fag or a harbour winch?
And from which is rum distilled – sugar cane or beet?

What is the product of limestone, soda and sand?
Who rode Aldaniti to Grand National fame?
Which boxing champ's surname means a firebrand?
And where did lacrosse begin as a proper game?

What word is used to describe a hare's home?
Who said the lungs of London are in Regent's Park?
Where in the world is sited the largest dome?
And which bird did Noah first release from the ark?

So how would you concoct a Black Russian to drink?
If you know all the answers, then you're in the pink.

Footnote: This sonnet invites you to pursue your own research. . . .

SONNET TO INERTIA

You've stopped – there's no movement – what do you do?
Check the duplex gauge and the current for traction;
Then, trying for reverse, you now have your cue,
Tripping and resetting after every action.

If it moves, reverse control governor cut-out switch;
If not, brake from the front while the guard drives from the rear.
With no backward movement, you still have a hitch,
So change the twenty-amp fuse behind your right ear.

No joy? Then go to the middle – open the FIS.
Try for reverse in rear of front part of the train.
If it goes, refuse at the front; if not, don't distress –
In front of rear unit, test for reverse again.

If it goes, guard drives from the rear with driver at front;
Otherwise, the train behind will give you a shunt!

Footnote: This sonnet relates to the workings of the Central Line Tube
stock on the London Underground.

SONNET TO SCHIZOPHRENIA

Being labelled 'schizoid' can be harsh and cruel –
Such a classification is a stigma.
Yet it is society that adds the fuel
For a condition that's still an enigma.

People are blinkered as to what is normal.
After all, behaviour is idiosyncratic.
But when we're embroiled in roles that are formal,
Our contrived comportment becomes automatic.

Sufferers are unable to come to terms
With the complexity of life and its forces;
Decisions of identity are wracked with germs
Leading to 'breakdowns' needing remedial courses.

So if being unaffected, though desirous to please,
Then I too am infected with this so-called disease.

SONNET TO PROCEDURE

If you are stopped at a signal that is red,
Assume there's a train in the section ahead.
If you identify the signal as automatic,
Then for one minute you will remain static.

If there's no apparent reason to be stopped,
Then perhaps the signal itself has flopped;
So tell your guard, apply the rule and trip past,
Not forgetting your whistle – give one long blast.

Proceed with extreme caution observing the track,
For there could be an obstruction or even a crack;
But what should be paramount in your mind
Is that another train you're most likely to find.

After passing two stop signals at clear or caution,
Resume normal speed and all details apportion.

Footnote: This sonnet relates to the workings of the Central Line Tube
stock on the London Underground.

SONNET TO CIRCUMSPECTION

The safety equipment throughout the train
Is there to protect the passengers and crew;
So do not treat any of it with disdain
Or harsh repercussions will alight on you.

The tripcock in effect is the driver's third eye;
The dead man, an insurance policy on his life.
The control governor is a bypass if his heart is awry,
And the audible warning acts like a nagging wife.

Like 'er indoors, all 'rules and regs' must be obeyed,
Especially when dealing with defective 'sticks';
For they need you only once to have strayed
And the depot above is where you'll get your kicks!

All speed restrictions make sure you heed,
And root out malpractice like a weed.

Footnote: This sonnet relates to the workings of the Central Line Tube stock on the London Underground.

SONNET TO ICONOCLASM

"Nothing is impossible," so many people chant;
The same call mishaps 'fate' when really they aren't.
You always hear "There's no such word as can't,"
But I've yet to see scientists create a plant.

To say that every cloud has a silver lining
Is often countered by another's defining;
For, as optimism supplants a pessimist's whining,
'All that glitters is not gold' is its undermining.

Honesty's the best policy, societies are taught,
While magnates exploit people, paying them less than they ought.
Yet mental happiness is the paradigm that is sought;
But when you're hungry, mind over matter amounts to nought.

The only maxim that will never sell anyone short
Is 'Life is what you make it' – now the ball is in your court.

SONNET TO MISADVENTURE

Hillsborough was awful – being asphyxiated,
Crushed so that you cannot draw breath.
Though football votaries are vituperated,
They did not deserve the incubus of death.

Being cremated alive must be just as horrid,
As happened at the Bradford and King's Cross fires –
Suffering a heat that is intolerably torrid,
As if being incinerated on human pyres.

The Clapham train crash and the Zeebrugge sinking
Are two more tragic cases of supernal acts.
Mortality's propinquity is like eyes blinking –
It strikes, despite us walking to avoid the cracks.

Like the Lockerbie plane blast – a cruel fiasco.
Ah, dinner is served. Could you pass the Tabasco!

SONNET TO ESCHATOLOGY

Human existence is like a seething ocean,
Where each of us is caught in a tide of time;
And as we angle to vent our own emotion,
We tread water to dodge the undertow of slime.

The slime that's failure, penury and rejection –
Also indiscriminately known as fate –
So that while swimming in one's chosen direction,
Ensure that your life jacket does not deflate.

As our voyage through life most of us can plot,
Spare a thought for the flotsam that is strewn.
It represents people that fortune's forgot,
For God cannot know everybody's tune.

But 'God' has ambiguous connotations,
Least being the reason for our complications.

SONNET TO INQUEST

The Prisoner does not need explaining –
Only the reason why it was made.
It was supposed to be entertaining
With the prospect of making the Grade*.

That an individual is suppressed
And heckled like a Hyde Park speaker
Does not imply a moral content
Or enjoin us to be a freedom seeker.

The context of the series is so diffuse
That interpretations are bound to abound;
But the underlying thread can well induce
Solicitude for an answer to be found.

For me it delineates what we could find
If our acquiescence is seen to be blind.

*Reference to Lew Grade, ITV supremo.

SONNET TO SPORT

In American football, what is a 'sack'?
And how many points for a rugby-league try?
What do we mean by the yachting term 'tack'?
Which weight precedes welter – light, feather or fly?

Name the apparatus where Randolphs are seen
And give me the height of a badminton net.
Which Wimbledon record's held by Billie Jean,
And in squash what's meant by the call of 'no set'?

Who ran the first sub-three-minute-fifty mile?
And when did Naismith invent basketball?
Who would you see practising the Sheffield style?
In which gruelling race would you 'hit the wall'?

What's the middle name of Sebastian Coe?
And which sport could you witness in a dojo?

Answers to 'Sonnet to Sport'

A 'sack' is the American term for a tackle.

A rugby-league try scores four points.

'Tacking' is when the craft's direction is changed to suit the wind vector.

Lightweight precedes welterweight in boxing categories.

Randolphs (and Rudolphs) require a trampoline.

A badminton net is five feet high.

Billie Jean King's Wimbledon record of most titles (twenty) has since been equalled by Martina Navratilova.

The call of 'no-set' at eight all in a game of squash is now obsolete, replaced by American scoring up to eleven.

The first sub-three-minutes-fifty-seconds mile was run by New Zealander John Walker.

Basketball was devised in the US circa 1891.

Sheffield style is practised by cyclists.

You could 'hit the wall' in the marathon around the twenty-two-mile mark.

Sebastian *Newbold* Coe, currently IOC chairman.

A 'dojo' houses the bouts between sumo wrestlers.

SONNET TO TERGIVERSATION

Policies are invented to guide humanity,
To keep it in check and afford it protection;
Morals are propounded to assuage our vanity
Like subterfuge designed to win an election.

The dissemination of rights bombards our ears,
With everyone proclaiming their modus vivendi;
Yet when our dictum does not gain three cheers,
Our tolerance evaporates like a warm brandy.

Often we're dyslectic when reading life's script,
Searching the scenario for our own appearance;
And with our role transposed the cue can be gripped
To dispassionately try to make a clearance.

Mankind's autopilot is selfish and purblind –
Only by switching to manual can we be kind.

SONNET TO BABEL

Throughout life we're examined and assessed,
And if accepted we are rubber-stamped,
Unless perchance we happen to be blessed
With the hedonist style of not being cramped.

For most, pigeonholing is our lot –
The riff-raff, nouveau riche, the middle classes –
Constantly updating what we've got;
Shenanigans comparable to stage farces.

We're in a one-act play without intermission
Where the assignment of roles depends on our brogue;
The script is a brouhaha of precondition
Where burgeoning stars are preoccupied with vogue.

It's naïve to believe life balances out –
Until we're dead – then everyone has nowt!

SONNET TO DRIVEL

Arty-farty,
Cheap and tarty;
Hocus-pocus,
Out of focus.

Mumbo jumbo,
Disney's Dumbo;
Flimflam, jim-jams,
Battering rams.

Tittle-tattle,
Baby's rattle;
Wishy-washy,
Wet and sloshy.

Hoodoo, Hogmanay;
Voodoo, Judgement Day.

SONNET TO GOBBLEDEGOOK

Poppycock, twaddle;
Cosset, mollycoddle.
Hubble-bubble,
Rabble and rubble.

Claptrap and piffle,
Hoedown and skiffle;
Hokum, hugger-mugger,
Harum-scarum, rugger.

Rickety, topsy-turvy,
Beriberi, scurvy;
Fiasco, willy-nilly,
Debacle, silly billy.

Scrimshank, pell-mell,
Schism, what the hell!

A MUSING SONNET

The gusting wind rouses me
From my nocturnal reverie;
In prospect lies another day –
Will it be bright or shades of grey?

The ball's in my court, I suppose,
As I dress in my dreary clothes.
Breakfasting on cereals, toast and honey,
I imagine being served by a Playboy bunny.

Nevertheless, reality hits home
As I scour the bathroom for a comb;
But does it matter that I'm hirsute?
Respect for appearance is a point that's moot.

After all, Bob Geldof became a 'Sir',
Even though he looks like a shaggy cur!

PACHYDERM'S SONNET

Being an elephant sure is not easy;
It's not a life to which humans can relate.
Even the park wardens make us queasy
With hypodermic darts that leave us sedate.

They tag and examine us while we're stunned,
Then monitor us from dawn until dusk.
I know it's better than cruelly being gunned
By people who want to cut off a tusk.

Mankind is also ruining our larder,
Draining our rivers and uprooting our trees,
And finding a mate is becoming harder
As friends are deported – to zoos, if you please.

As mammals we're unique with four knees and a trunk,
But sometimes I wish that I'd been born as a skunk!

SONNET OF ELEGY

In the days when elephants abounded,
Hunters shot them because they were there;
But now their lifestyle has been confounded
By poachers who do not flinch a hair.

Whether for ivory or just the sport,
Elephants are expendable, it seems;
And even when callous killers are caught,
They claim they're merely realising their dreams.

Amid the mercenary morass of greed,
Pedlars see ivory as the road to riches.
The only deterrent such scum will heed –
Used as under-soil heating for football pitches!

We must not abuse our domain over these mammals,
Or when water runs short will we persecute camels!

SONNET TO ARPEGGIO

Waffle, hogwash,
Tommyrot and tosh.
Farrago, fiddle-faddle,
Up the creek – no paddle.

Slipshod, slapdash,
Hotchpotch, mishmash.
Kowtow and gerrymander,
Hobnob; Save the Panda.

Helter-skelter, loop the loop,
Razzle-dazzle, flown the coop.
Hunky-dory, spick and span,
Busybody, Desperate Dan.

Dilly-dally, Aunt Sally,
Shilly-shally, a blind alley.

SONNET TO SCLEROSIS

Playing squash is important to me,
But, more than just participating,
The joy of winning essentially
Is worth all the expectorating.

Losing leaves you empty inside –
Piqued and devoid of self-esteem.
In contrast, triumph hoists your pride
And affirms your place in life's scheme.

It may be fine to be genial and meek
As Christianity expatiates,
But to me it's tosh – you're seen as weak,
A greenhorn everyone repudiates.

Victory's achieved by turning the screws,
Not the other cheek or you're bound to lose.

SONNET TO EXISTENTIALISM

Doing what's expected,
Saying what we ought,
Always being corrected
In word, deed and thought.

Our behaviour is modified
To think before we act,
So we'll have a smoother ride
Through life if we have tact.

Understanding human nature
Relies on conditional learning,
With familiar nomenclature
To enable our discerning.

We supplant instinct with pretension,
So we function without dissension.

SONNET TO SUSPENSION

To hang or not to hang,
That is the dangling dilemma.
Humanists would feel a pang
Seeing a body's last tremor.

'Good riddance' is surely what
Hardliners are bound to utter.
'They do not matter a jot,
Plus our jails they would not clutter.'

Yet do we have the right to kill
Someone who has callously slain;
Or is it wrong not to fulfil
Our duty to remove the stain.

Religious folk may forfend and hope,
But murderers only fear the rope.

SONNET TO PROVENANCE

Is committing suicide OK,
Or is it something we should scotch?
Do we have the moral right to say
God's plan for me is mine to botch?
Or are we obligated to play
Without the thought to stop our watch.

Self-destruction can be a trap
When you want to dispel despair,
Because here there is an overlap
Between not having any care
And the wish to start your final nap
To stop the pain that's always there.

But while there's seldom love in self-erasure,
Is it through love that we'd have euthanasia?

SONNET TO RECIPROCITY

Respect for a person, claimed Kant,
Should merit respect in return;
So that we react like a plant
Whose responses are easy to learn.

Though predictable in the main,
We require certain stimuli,
That's why if we suffer pain,
We resort to an eye for an eye.

But nothing is simply good or bad:
Every action is open to view.
Just like the meaning for the word 'mad'
Includes angry, deranged and 'cuckoo'!

Thus the semantics of interpretation
Fuels the philosophers' procrastination.

SONNET TO JEHOVAH'S WITLESS

I was sitting at home watching *M*A*S*H*
When a Jehovah's Witness rang the bell.
Before he could spout his balderdash,
I unsubtly told him to "Go to hell!"

"We don't believe in hell," he cried.
"I don't believe in God or heaven."
"Jehovah will not be denied. . . ."
"Scram! You've got to the count of seven."

"Don't you want to be redeemed?"
"Listen, mate, my life is my own."
"God's kingdom offers a life undreamed
Beyond any earthly pleasures known. . . ."

"That's simply piffle to exploit our plight;
Love conquers all, now get out of my sight!"

SONNET TO ADJUDICATION

The liberally minded dismiss the foetus
As nothing more than a clump of cells;
Anti-abortionists swear they will not beat us
And promptly toll all their alarm bells.

The central issue (if you'll pardon the pun)
Is whether it's moral to 'terminate';
Some say it's as if you use a gun
When the makings of life you extirpate.

Others state that it's a woman's right
To have dominion over her own flesh,
And that Catholic cant is a blight
Upon women whom they seek to enmesh.

While the woman's well-being is paramount,
Does it mean what's not seen doesn't count?

SONNET TO THE TRINITY

Committed Christians make the claim
That God is omniscient: all-knowing;
If that's so, then He knew the game
When Jesus Christ made His showing.

That God, His Son and the Holy Ghost
Are all one, is religious teaching;
Yet if Christ Himself proclaimed the boast,
The implications are far-reaching.

God created men that suffer pain,
So did it hurt by proxy on the Cross;
Or being God was He able to feign
And reconstitute Himself without loss.

If Christ was God and they each knew their fate,
Then with Christ being dead, God too is of late!

SONNET TO PROCREATION

The basic instinct of woman and man
Is for intercourse with one another;
Though the Church decrees we're all of one clan,
Yet bars sex between sister and brother.

So related in spirit but not in flesh,
It's permissible to spread our seed;
And when in thrall of a 'prophet' like Koresh,*
Then lust is sated according to need.

While the act is dressed up as love's consummation,
It's spoken of coarsely as 'dipping one's wick';
And when rapists do it to vent their frustration
Our righteous morality says they are sick.

Sex can be bestial but mainly benign,
Just like a mania you cannot define.

* A Davidian cult 'extinguished' by US military.

SONNET TO MEANING

Well-being is for what we strive,
Recognition is what we seek;
While neglect curbs our drive
And rebuttal makes us weak.

Belonging is an inbuilt need,
Since through it burgeons self-worth;
Without it our hearts will bleed
At not being the salt of the earth.

So being given a role to play
Is the essence of life's import,
Whereas not having ought to say
Will tend to see us falling short.

Wherever we eventually fit,
The problem becomes finding some kit.

SONNET TO PERSPECTIVE

Millions starving in the world today
And I'm thinking what to have for dinner;
With carnage sanctioned in the Gulf affray,
A blasphemer is condemned a sinner.

I curse when spilling tea on my trousers,
Yet thousands shuffle around in tatters;
Women have difficulty selecting blouses,
Oblivious to what in life really matters.

Men fret about acoustics in their car,
When hundreds of people around cannot hear.
Folk moan about cost at their local bar,
While hordes are so thirsty they can't shed a tear.

If what's important is saving our soul,
Then materialism is an own goal.

SONNET TO GAMMON

Glad rags, wiggle-waggle;
Party piece; barter, haggle.
Set-to, Dennis the Menace,
Hobnob, anyone for tennis?

Hurly-burly, hoi polloi,
Pinocchio, the real McCoy.
Hurdy-gurdy, powwow,
Paraphernalia, highbrow.

Razzmatazz, pitter-patter,
All that jazz, idle chatter.
Mealy-mouthed, wheeler-dealer,
Troubadour, faith healer.

Mayday, hullabaloo;
Let us pray, OK, I'm through.

SONNET TO MODALITY

Communities are orderly, almost tame,
Permitting us to live without hassle;
But if we err from the rules of the game,
Our fortress becomes a beach sandcastle.

In daily encounters, lip service we pay
And change is given in treatment in kind;
But if from accepted paths we stray,
Then the unpredictable we will find.

Through using others as sounding boards,
We learn to harmonise and follow suit;
And sometimes when we strike the wrong chords,
Inevitably we have the odd dispute.

Life's heuristic scheme would seem to suggest
We hearken to those who can have us blessed.

SONNET TO FLUMMERY

Jingo, lingo; show-stopper,
Jag, zigzag, come a cropper.
Wheeze, striptease, camiknickers,
Cholesterol, dodgy tickers.

Cloak-and-dagger, hush-hush,
Double-dealing, royal flush.
Gibberish, nitty-gritty,
Baloney, Bristol City.

Skulduggery, hanky-panky,
Raggle-taggle, swish and swanky.
Lovey-dovey, well-wisher,
Lah-di-dah, kingfisher.

Bumbledom, buckshee, tee-hee,
Sitting pretty, me and Rosie Lee.

SONNET TO PROSODY

My first is in mirror, but not in reflection;
The second is alpha if you're Greek;
The next is heard at a dentist's inspection;
The fourth is in pinch, but not in tweak.

Again has the fifth, but not encore;
The sixth is a vowel multiplied by two;
The next is silently said in whore;
Bingo has the eighth – shout 'House' if you do!

With crumpets the next two are served at the Ritz;
The eleventh crops up in wassails, twice;
The twelfth is salient in knockers not tits;
The penultimate features in fee and price.

Reading, writing, 'rithmetic, each has the last;
After this girl was moulded they broke the cast.

SONNET TO ENCOMIUM

Undeniably pretty,
Indisputably fine,
With the perspicacity
Of fortified wine.

Irrefutably svelte,
Unmistakeably nice,
Her body makes me melt
Like a sheet of pack ice.

Flawlessly shaped,
Irrefrangibly crowned,
And, when undraped,
In her beauty I'm drowned.

With a visage perfectly fashioned,
I'm irrevocably impassioned.

SONNET TO VERNACULAR

So you think you know all about the city,
With its bustling brokers, stags, bulls and bears,
About selling short and then sitting pretty
If the price drops on the respective shares.

Are you familiar with wily White Squires
And White Knights that can foil a hostile bid?
Did you know a concert party 'conspires',
While a fan club maintains it never did?

Are you aware of unit trusts' subtle 'spread'
And of traded options, 'puts' and 'calls'?
Do you know what is meant by 'breakfast and bed'
And the upshot when the Footsie falls?

Or is your comprehension that of Sid –
With the perception of a dustbin lid?

SONNET TO DOLOUR

Life can be easy and life can be hard;
It can make you happy, but also glum.
And life can be runny like heated lard,
Or like a song with no words – so you hum.

What does it matter when folk blether
About insignificant tribulations?
Who cares about the wretched weather
And electioneering proclamations?

Fulfilment is what ultimately counts,
Whether it's real or imaginary;
For a ton of wealth is not worth an ounce
When it is time to board Death's ferry.

So when despondency prompts my complaining,
Don't piss down my back and tell me it's raining.

SONNET TO DEBEE

Irresistible is your shapely form
That adulation is herein required;
Its amplitude defies the norm
And never palls when viewed unattired.

Your consummate beauty provokes titillation
With a sweetness that is never cloying;
Thus my libido derives some mitigation
For a baseness that I find annoying.

Your prim but protean conformation
Panders to man's immutable vice;
But beneath your outré presentation,
I discern that you're jocund and nice.

Though your smile may inveigle my fervid praise,
I'm grateful you puncture my mawkish malaise.

SONNET TO OBLOQUY

The meaning of *The Prisoner* is patent enough:
It amounts to a story of ingenious bluff.
The image is fostered of a man oppressed
And the individualism he seeks to wrest.

But he is recalcitrant and non-conforming –
In fact his character is quite heart-warming.
He embodies our image of a system-breaker,
But actually emerges as just a dream-maker.

That someone can exist amidst any state
And retain untarnished their unique persona,
Is only possible if you can dictate
Imperceptively from a green-domed cupola!

The Prisoner's an exercise in questioning reason,
Where incorrect answers are interpreted as treason.

SONNET TO SAMANTHA

Once upon a time there was a chit
Who pined continuously for success;
Then one day for snapshots she did sit,
Willingly topless, not under duress.

Eventually, as a precocious seventeen-year-old,
A newspaper featured her desquamation;
In a matter of months, history did unfold
And she became etched in men's contemplation.

Her dishabille would infatuate hordes –
Her following eclipsed even that of the Queen –
Irredeemably enamoured by her gourds,
Upon which, metaphorically, they did wean.

Inflation is not only Maggie Thatcher's claim –
Samantha Fox can also say it made her name.

SONNET TO PROPENSITY

Why am I standing here,
Waiting so patiently
For someone to appear –
A stage celebrity.

And when finally she comes,
Sheepishly I approach.
I'm all fingers and thumbs
As my request I broach:

I ask for an autograph.
She demurely turns round;
There's a hint of a laugh –
But she signs without sound.

Her being puts fabric in my cloth;
She is the lantern, me the moth.

SONNET TO EXEGESIS

I'm a philosopher; I'm worldly-wise –
I can offer impartial advice.
Trust me because I won't tell any lies
And my judgement is as cold as ice.

Raise any topic you like at all
And I'll give you an unbiased view;
By my answers I will stand or fall,
For my detachment vouchsafes what's true.

Abortion – right of mother, right to life.
Suicide – self-possession or despair.
Euthanasia – humane release from strife.
Animal rights – misplaced concern, welfare.

Punishment – justice or retribution.
The meaning of life – circumlocution.

SONNET TO DESPOND

A deadbeat, done for, out of sorts,
Disenchanted and dismayed,
Discredited in and on the courts,
Defeated by those you've played.

Lost in a vacuum of self-disgust
With all meaning gone to blazes,
Each day you bathe in a putrid must,
Since life no longer amazes.

All is irrelevant round and about
When you don't have any bearing;
It's pointless to argue or even shout
Because you're just beyond caring.

If hope ever leaves Pandora's box,
Then it means you've scoffed all the chocs!

SONNET TO QUIZZING

In what sport could you catch a crab?
How many hoops are used in croquet?
Which Swedish boxer had a famous jab?
And where would you be if you drank Tokay?

What's the distinction of Bruce Hobbs, the jockey?
How many hurdles in the 400 metres?
Which term is used to start a game of hockey?
And who were World Cup clubmates of Martin Peters?

Curling has a slitter; what does hurling use?
Which countries compete for the Calcutta Cup?
How many Wimbledon matches did Borg lose?
And where would you expect to see a tup?

Lastly, when were the Ashes first contested?
And with whom would a swizzle stick be invested?

Answers to 'Sonnet to Quizzing'

Rowing – catching a crab is when the blade of the oar merely skims the water's surface.

Croquet features six hoops.

Ingemar Johansson (also known as 'Ingo's bingo').

You would most likely be in Hungary.

Bruce Hobbs was the youngest Grand National winner (on Battleship).

There are ten hurdles in the men's 400-metres race.

Still started with a 'bully-off'!

Bobby Moore and Geoff Hurst were the West Ham teammates of Martin Peters.

Trick question! Curling has a 'stone', hurling has a projectile called a sliotar.

England and Scotland compete for the Calcutta Cup in rugby union (as part of the Six Nations competition).

Bjorn Borg only lost four times at Wimbledon.

In a field – it's an uncastrated male sheep.

The Ashes were first contested in 1882–3 between Australia and England.

A barman would use it to mix cocktails.

SONNET TO IMPLORATION

"Let, please – I couldn't see the ball."
"No let; 8–6, match ball from the right."
"But, marker, what about my call?"
"Your own bad position caused your plight."
"No, my opponent's stance obscured the wall,
Delaying my response to the ball's flight."
"Please resume play and stop trying to stall –
In any event, the ball was too tight."

"Can I appeal? I think you're being severe.
The ball was loose – floating like a kite."
"Appeal rejected; you were nowhere near,
Even if you had had a clear sight."

"Yes, but—" "Continue or a point I shall dock."
"But—" "Point – game and match I award to Fred Cock!"

SONNET TO MARIA

My addiction is crass, yet I'm starkly bemused
And enthralled by your incomparable physique.
Though my regard is aesthetic, I'm still accused
Of salacious leering, despite my critique.

Dreaming of the exfoliation of your robes
Is a reverie that propitiates a carnal lust;
Having my face beleaguered by your bulging globes
Would incite sheer ecstasy while being an insensate must.

This expatiation elucidates my intense rapture,
Without resorting to Rabelaisian terms of detraction;
For though your bodily phenomena induced my capture,
Your endearing diffidence escapes my primeval infraction.

Your figure is the paradigm of womanly perfection,
The quintessence of beauty – a miracle of conception.

SONNET TO DIALECTIC

We're told to value all human life
And that it always must be protected,
Yet we find that abortion is rife
So are the premises disconnected?

Women are accorded complete control
Over their bodies to do as they please,
And thus a foetus is put on parole
Or else expelled as no more than a sneeze.

If the baby's a tenant with a right to exist,
Surely it's callous to have it 'evicted';
But if it's considered as an unwanted cyst,
Then on it no pain can there be inflicted.

The ethics of abortion are invariably lost
In the trade-off of logic for emotional cost.

SONNET TO GALLIMAUFRY

Positivism – just what is that?
Another word to corral our views.
Subjectivism – this sounds flat,
But means from within come our cues.

Emotivism – that rings a bell;
It's all about our gut reaction.
Rationalism – now, here's hard sell;
Being logical is its attraction.

Fundamentalism – this seems grand,
Though Salman Rushdie would disagree!
Secularism is the latest brand,
Where it all boils down to you and me.

So what will be tomorrow's buzzword?
Expedientism, or is that absurd?

SONNET TO EVALUATION

Are we puppets or human beings,
Here to justify our deeds?
Or merely to satisfy needs
By using others as our means?

Are we beasts driven by urges
Which when sated reappear,
Leaving our destiny unclear
As to when our true self emerges?

Are we as individuals free,
Or culturally homogenised
And taught what's best and to be prized
So that we know when to agree?

The questions depend on implication;
The answers rest with our expectation.

SONNET TO FRUSTRATION

Triviality rules; pettiness reigns.
Splitting hairs is all the rage;
Bureaucracy gives us mental pains –
Dotting the i's on every page.

Permission for this, sanction for that;
Always someone to whom we pander.
So much hot air, yet still I'm left flat
Listening to people gerrymander.

The power to act is tied in red tape
Purposely, so we all toe the line.
Such pettifogging leaves me agape,
But defiance merely exacts a fine!

The stifling mesh of social interaction
Can easily cause man's putrefaction.

SONNET TO DISPENSATION

Now I have got time to spare,
I have no excuse not to write;
Yet there's still nothing to declare
And the horizon is no more bright.

Of course I will not despair
Because the tunnel end brings light;
But I seem to have shed all care
That it matters what follows night.

With the threads of life laid bare,
It's just a balance of pain and delight;
But that doesn't mean it's fair –
Rather that it's simply black and white.

However we fare, whatever we might,
Never lose faith in what you believe's right.

SONNET TO INDIVIDUATION

The Prisoner and its meaning
May leave you tied up in knots,
And with every further screening
You'll be taking Valium shots.

But there exists an antidote
To bring you down to earth:
When next you're called upon to vote,
Just consider what it's worth.

It's not really freedom that's in dispute,
Or the belief we each have a shout.
What truly matters, as for King Canute,
Is that our presence removes self-doubt.

Our meaning can only be underlined
By the parameters that have us confined.

SONNET TO FLATULENCE

What is there in life to hold me
And repulse the angst of despair?
Is there anybody who has told me
About Heidegger's attitude of 'care'?

Is there reason to believe in living
The contingency of what I decide,
Or was Sartre essentially giving
An indeterminate ticket to ride?

Do I need a God for consolidation,
As Kant thought it rational to surmise,
Or was Hume right in his extrapolation
That good is but survival in disguise?

Am I lost in Mill's 'liberty' to be my own man,
Or have I found Moore's fallacy to cramp life's game plan?

SONNET TO IRRESOLUTION

Afghanistan is a country scarred
By people who simply do not belong;
Yet since terrorists have not been barred,
Nato forces seek to right a wrong.

Troops are deployed to purge the land,
But chasing shadows is their vain fate.
Victims fall prey to traps in the sand,
While politicians prevaricate.

Some countries are steeped in tribal lore
And will not conform unless overrun;
So can you cut out a cankered core
And leave the apple to grow in the sun?

Until we resolve to treat the tree,
From evil the fruit will not be free.

SONNET TO VERISIMILITUDE

Truth is all that I perceive,
Until it's proven otherwise.
For though I may be given lies,
It's not for me to self-deceive.

The truth is all that I believe
Of everything before my eyes;
And even as each image dies,
In memory has its reprieve.

Truth is that to which I cleave
As the essence to make me wise,
And yet from error I cannot rise
Until fallibility takes its leave.

Within my mind the truth is secure,
But when I speak it becomes impure.

SONNET TO PRETENCE

Is existentialism cool,
Or merely constipated claptrap?
Was Sartre playing the fool,
Or intent on getting a back-slap?

Yet he refused the Nobel Prize,
So perhaps he was sincere;
But then, many have told lies
To allay a perceived fear.

Being is the crux of the matter,
Which is translated from choice;
Though you needn't be the Mad Hatter
To know Alice was Carroll's voice.

If we are what we do and thus become,
It's a case of who has the loudest drum.

SONNET TO PRESENCE

Floor-walking in a Tesco store
Is a mind-numbing bore –
In fact, it's a binding chore.

You're looked upon as a ninny,
A jumped-up guard in a pinny.
Just an emasculated hinny.

From wines and spirits to home 'n' wear,
Tediously traipsing here and there –
Trudging miles to get nowhere.

And when you're sought for help,
It's to search for someone's whelp –
As much fun as chewing kelp.

If self-respect is important to me,
I may just as well be Tweedledee.

SONNET TO THRENODY

Those of us assembled here
Are a witness to Dominic's life:
It contained many a day of cheer,
But was also riddled with strife.

He played an excellent game of chess,
And liked nothing more than to read;
The knowledge he amassed would impress,
Meantime gardening fulfilled a need.

Then an affliction plagued his mind,
And illness ravaged his health.
Yet no one better could you find,
For consideration was his wealth.

While his body lies here in decay,
His true essence will not pass away.

SONNET TO ATARAXIA

I'm endowed with consciousness to know how I feel,
But realising I exist is no big deal.
On the contrary, it seems it is nature's bent
To make me aware of life's intent.

When I'm fed, dressed, sheltered and out of the cold,
What else is there that I need to hold?
How am I different from a grooming chimpanzee
Or superior to a pollen-seeking busy bee?

It appears I've evolved to think of myself as me
So that I understand how others might see;
And thus conformity ensures I can survive
By learning when to depart and arrive.

So glorifying a life encumbered by thought
Is like bothering with sums that all come to nought.

SONNET TO DEVIATION

What is pleasure but imagined delight,
Recognised by all through smiling faces?
By the same token, depressive cases
Are surely born of a chimeric plight.

So life as we see it awaits our palette,
There to be coloured in manifold hues;
But this analogy is not news,
Except when the brush becomes a mallet.

Just like art by some is defined as kitsch,
Others assert it reflects our condition;
And while some claim it surmounts inhibition,
Cynics will still decry life as a glitch.

In this world there are artists, models and viewers,
Which makes life a contrast of dreamers and doers.

SONNET TO APODOSIS

All that I know about life I perceive;
Nothing is dreamt that I do not know.
So why when there's death do we need to grieve,
When others would say it was time to go?

Experience is the foundation on which we build
And reason is the mortar to cement our acts;
So why should a liar be called weak-willed
Just because the truth is shorn of facts?

Such values are not given; nor are they found.
They're created to sublimate our mundane being.
So why kid ourselves that we are all bound
By anything other than our own decreeing?

We evoke the meaning that befits our cause
To erase life's banality with applause.

SONNET TO APPURTENANCE

Religion or science – which has the answers?
Wherein lies the truth we want to know?
Both tantalise us like striptease dancers
In that they reveal more than they show.

One uses rationale, the other revelation,
Yet both pose problems for the human condition:
It's either Big Bang and random permutation
Or divine creation and the threat of perdition.

While evolution explains how we have become,
It affords no suggestion for what we should be,
Which makes acting correctly just a rule of thumb
That's reached arbitrarily because we agree.

Our being demands more than knowledge and facts –
It requires sentience, which science lacks.

SONNET TO QUIXOTISM

Life is much simpler when
We do not get embroiled
In analysing now and then
Why our plans are often foiled.

We're not made for idle thinking,
Mulling over life's big purpose,
For then we're like a car pinking
With a mixture that is surplus.

When the road ahead is clear,
Then there is no need for choices;
But a life devoid of fear
Just invokes our restive voices.

It seems life without choosing amounts to nought,
Yet with it comes wanting, and that can be fraught.

SONNET TO AMBER

Sent from heaven, a forlorn soul,
Too perfect, even for God.
She wandered in search of a role
Until from me she got the nod.

To say she craved attention
Would be less than she deserved;
Rather it is my contention
She revelled in being observed.

Always keen to playfully scurry
In pursuit of whatever stirred;
At other times there was no hurry,
And upon me she settled and purred.

She endeared with her infectious verve,
So what purpose did her demise serve?

SONNET TO ACQUITTAL

I'm not bothered about life –
It just seems a dreary drag.
Why endure such pointless strife?
I'll simply raise the white flag.

If you tell me I'm wrong – OK,
It boosts your ego, no doubt,
But I know all things are grey,
That's why I don't need to shout.

Being alive is the easy part;
Believing is much harder to do.
For I'm sure it's all a false start,
So it doesn't matter who wins through.

The fact that it does belies the fiction –
The plain truth is that life's an addiction.

SONNET TO PRESUMPTION

"I know nothing," Socrates surely said.
Added Plato, "Except forms in my head."
"Matter matters," opined Aristotle –
Though you won't find a thinking bottle.

While Augustine averred faith as his roof,
Aquinas set God in logic for proof
Until Descartes declared, "We need both
Before to knowledge we can betroth."

Then Spinoza shouts, "Pantheism's the key."
Yet empiricist John Locke won't agree.
Hume holds that mere impressions be our fount,
But Kant claims his 'imperative' must count.

If now you see sense in the Grand Design,
Then you'll believe this is the bottom line.

SONNET TO SOPHIE

Hobbes hailed life as 'nasty, brutish and short',
   While Berkeley said it was all in the mind.
Rousseau reckoned that culture should be fought
   And then innately we'd revert to being kind.

Hegel romanticised God as 'idea',
   While Voltaire vaunted, "He's invented!"
Nietzsche killed off God without fear,
   And Darwin had his good name dented.

Then Marx motioned for drastic upheaval,
   While Mill moved to maximise pleasure.
Sartre thought 'choosing' was man's last retrieval,
   But Russell ruled maths as life's measure.

Falsification was the answer for Popper,
Till Derrida deconstructed – came a cropper!

SONNET TO NORMA

Portering might seem facile,
But requires an orderly approach;
And that's where I had a good coach
Who guided me down every aisle.

Norma took me under her wing,
Showed me which bins to pack,
How to stack on a rack
And what's meant by a box with string.

Picking soon became a piece of cake –
From Barbies to Bosch drills and bits,
Chocolate factories to cupboard kits,
Yet oddly never a garden rake.

But the highlight of Argos for me
Was when Norma's singing reached top C.

SONNET TO EXCORIATION

When your guys are cut and the wind takes hold,
Expect some buffeting to ensue;
And although they say fate favours the bold,
Believe me when I say it's not true.

If cast adrift, you're easily forgotten
And time subsumes you like a disease.
Inertia then turns your brain to cotton
And life becomes a jangle of keys.

Yet experience of life is what counts,
So doing nothing will not add up –
Unlike backing the Grand National mounts
That might come home in the Martell Cup.

But when the anticlimax of knowing bites,
Life becomes a succession of empty rites.

SONNET TO DISABUSAL

I've concluded *The Prisoner*'s a myth
Because the premise has a flaw;
It's like trying to extract the pith
From a tree that's become a door.

Like Alice's abstruse rule forty-two,
Which enforces a height restriction,
The Prisoner presumes it's his due
To be quizzed about dereliction.

In truth, when society's disowned
You're a captive of the periphery,
So having your alter ego rezoned
Is like a corpse doing midwifery.

The series may well be an analogy,
But for me it's turned into an allergy.

SONNET TO ANTICLIMAX

The exciting expectation
Of seeing lush Liz Hurley's
Sharpe manifestation
Tickled my short and curlies.

The crimped corsage of her dress
Caused her bosom to balloon –
Bare skin invited a caress
That within me played a tune.

When ordered to show her wares,
She lowered her bodice of lace;
But just as the pips of her pears
Appeared, the film panned to her face.

A blurred glimpse of her darling buds
Hardly lathered my carnal suds.

SONNET TO INTERFACE

It's pedestrian driving buses,
But your concentration must be sharp,
For other motorists' mad rushes
Could leave them playing St Peter's harp.

You need patience when pensioners tarry,
Tolerance when kids play with the bell,
Diplomacy when passengers harry
And stoicism when drivers give you hell.

Though it's tedious issuing fares –
Rovers, singles, returns and bus-riders –
There's a knack to showing someone cares
When it comes down to transport providers.

While in St Christopher's care I'm thrust,
I enjoy airing my wanderlust.

SUCCINCT SONNET

Having, doing,
Being, knowing.
Seeing, wooing,
Coming, going.

Enjoying this,
Enduring that.
Taking the piss,
Exchanging a chat.

Chasing around
From A to B;
Testing for sound
With doh, ray, me.

All to use time,
Just like this rhyme.

SONNET TO VELLEITY

If life has no sustainable pleasures,
Then why should I endure tribulation?
There have to be undiscovered treasures
In order to inspire motivation.

Being successful at squash competition
Requires effort to procure any gain;
This is a bearable precondition,
Provided it is not always in vain.

And when inactivity leaves me vacant,
It's imperative to gaze upon beauty;
For without experience I'm forsakened
And consigned to the tedium of duty.

All I want is a palatable slice of life
Without having to cut myself on the knife.

SONNET TO IMMISCIBILITY

If we're all alone in this universe,
Then what a waste of space!
Or is the mystery God's curse
To blight the human race?

Yet if God exists for sure,
We would take life as read;
Doing good might be a bore,
But then we're a long time dead.

Conversely, do we need God at all,
Since the cosmos is self-contained
And its randomness seems to forestall
The idea it was preordained?

Although science provides the facts,
It's religion that pays the tax.

SONNET TO SCIOLISM

Can true happiness be obtained
Or is it just 'peace of mind'?
For whatever we have ingrained
It stays elusive to find.

While achievements provide the sauce
To keep our interests alive,
It's recognition that is the main course
That allows ourselves to thrive.

Yet when fulfilment begins to fade
And vicarious pleasures peter,
It is memories that keep us staid
When they register on our meter.

Though we ply the present and play the future,
It's the past that binds them like a suture.

SONNET TO MY PARAMOUR

Your beige-blue eyes bewitch me
Like a rabbit caught in a car's glare;
Your soft-spoken words enrich me,
So forgive me if I seem to stare.

What magnetism permeates my soul
When your body lies close to mine!
It's as if my half becomes whole,
Forming something truly divine.

Your breasts so proud, your thighs so tender
And in between such golden splendour:
With these delights to charm my gender,
I offer you complete surrender.

No subornation could take the place
Of one osculation face-to-face.

SONNET D'AMOUR

What is love that has us bound
Like convoluted strands?
Yet I'm glad that I have found
Someone to clasp my hands.

Folks say that opposites attract,
And I certainly can't resist
The incontrovertible fact
That it was heaven when we kissed.

While your candy kisses ignite me,
Your sweet caress cannot be denied;
And though intimacy does excite me,
Just being with you keeps me satisfied.

It seems my life has been in stasis,
But now I've found a lush oasis.

SONNET TO CONSUMMATION

Nothing can ever rival
Two people coming together –
Not even a sherry trifle
Or sizzling, sunshiny weather.

Can ecstasy be defined
In terms of human glory,
Or is it all in the mind
Just like a fairy-tale story?

What love a woman must feel
When allowing a man inside,
And for him it is the seal
Of an emotion he can't hide.

Such union is poetry in motion,
An expression of true devotion.

SONNET TO SINGULARITY

True love is like the sun –
It can blot out everyone;
And, when all's said and done,
Like ice cream it starts to run.

True love is all-embracing –
It sets our hearts a-racing
And in its shockproof casing
No part can be abasing.

True love does not have a prize
Or value that one can surmise.
It even bemuses the wise
Because it carries no disguise.

True love cannot be denied,
For then it wouldn't have applied.

SONNET MONDIAL

Football champions France were brought down to earth
By Senegal playing out of their skins;
Then Poland and Portugal suffered stillbirth
When South Korea gained dramatic wins.

Argentina's sly efforts were trumped
With Beckham's penalty for a foul;
Italy were ignominiously dumped,
As were Spain with a lacklustre Raúl.

Inexorably, Germany progressed,
Mopping up all the giant-killers;
While Brazil left England second best
With Rivaldo and Cafu their pillars.

In the final Brazil's brilliance bore fruit
And Ronaldo's reward – the Golden Boot.

World Cup, 2002

SONNET TO CONCUPISCENCE

Why do men have to cleave
To a woman – they know not whom?
Where is the need to conceive,
Just because she harbours a womb?

What is the impulse to 'get lucky'
Solely to sate a sexual urge?
How can Catholics think it mucky
When procreation escapes their purge?

How is the fabric of love explained,
Even when the stitching becomes frayed?
What advantage purports to be gained
While blindly seeing nature's obeyed?

Can we not see each other as one
Whose integrity needs not be undone?

SONNET TO APORIA

We are born without an inkling
Of what life may have in store,
Except for a genetic sprinkling
That affects what goes before.

Growing up is selfish in nature
As defined by our need to survive;
Then we adopt a nomenclature
Which provides reasons for being alive.

Whether Christian, Muslim, Jew or Rasta,
We wrap our choices with good intent;
But just like sauces that souse our pasta,
We end up doing what's expedient.

So if life's as easy to understand,
Then why do we seek the promised land?

SONNET TO FIDELITY

I may listen to the lyrics of others,
But your song is the one that I sing;
And when something heavy my spirit smothers,
It lifts me up like an angel's wing.

Essaying to put my finger on love
Is like attempting to catch the wind;
But as salient as the stars above,
I'd be rich if I could have it tinned.

Although my feelings defy depiction,
Like trying to draw the infinity of space,
I'm certain of my heartfelt conviction
That we can be a team in the human race.

So knowing my love was never a whim,
I pledge you my future, Angela Kim.

SONNET TO EPIPHANY

Writing this is churning me,
So please bear with me while I labour.
You may think you've set me free,
But I felt prodded by a sabre.

You know I'd walk the plank for you
And swim in shark-infested water;
I'd even start to come on cue
And then pretend to like your daughter.

Perhaps our love became too cloying,
In which case I was quite naïve:
I could not see we were enjoying
Something others could not believe.

I only hope that you'll recall
Why a climbing plant needs a wall.

SONNET TO REVERSION

Does anybody need another
To accompany them through this life,
Or do we only call our brother
When we encounter grief or strife?

When we choose from the opposite sex,
What exactly are we looking for?
Is it an ideal like Posh and Becks,
Or a fumbling fling upon the floor?

When people can be taken or left
Like vegetables picked from a stall,
Then our humanity becomes bereft
Of the feelings that hold us in thrall.

If Hell is other people, as Sartre said,
Then we may as well paint the whole world red.

SONNET TO COMPLAISANCE

I make her happy,
I make her mad.
I make her snappy,
I make her glad.

I make her drink,
I make her cry.
I make her think,
I make her sigh.

I make her moan,
Laugh and whimper;
I make her groan,
Smile and simper.

Above all, I've made her,
And I wouldn't trade her.

SONNET TO SACRIFICE

If God exists, then face the fact
He's insecure and quite self-serving;
He opts to keep Himself intact
By sending someone undeserving.
Thus Christ's calling made an impact,
Yet *his* suffering was unnerving;
And so the grace that we all lacked
Became for us all life-preserving.

That is if there is a hereafter
Where all worldly wrongs are righted;
But if not then there's nothing dafter
Than with God's burden being blighted,
Because existence devoid of laughter
Is ultimately so short-sighted.

SONNET TO ATTESTATION

I've known Roy ever since squash was cool,
And between us we've slid on many courts;
All along he's been nobody's fool
And has never been caught without his shorts.

How Roy and Erica got together
Seems to me a propitious turn of fate.
But what's certain – they're birds of a feather,
And now need a nest to conjugate.

Whatever the future may have in store,
They know they will have each other's backing;
And whether or not they're married in law,
It's clear that love will never be lacking.

So drink to their health and then toast their bond,
That of each other they'll always be fond.

SONNET TO VEXATION

What irritations can we number
That could make a person ratty?
For instance when we're so near slumber
Why does our spouse become chatty?

Untying a shoelace that becomes a knot;
Paying tax for feckless job-seekers' dole;
TV presenters who care not a jot
And talk over programmes as the credits roll.

People who park in a no-waiting zone;
A leaking pen found in your coat pocket;
The irksome music played on the phone
That makes you yank the lead from the socket.

Being shellacked playing squash really grates,
But apart from that I have no hates!

SONNET TO SYNCHRONICITY

Love is nebulous, some may say,
Just like a cloud that swamps your mind;
You never know the time of day
Because to all your heart is blind.

Is love driven by a desirous urge
To fulfil the need to copulate,
Or can something more noble emerge
Where spirituality can dictate?

What makes two people feel in tune
As if their paths were meant to meet?
It seems to love we're not immune,
And with it life is made replete.

Physical attraction may be the start,
But relationships flourish from the heart.

SONNET TO QUIDDITY

Bursting a prize balloon,
Singing out of tune,
Dropping a sticky spoon.

Contracting a disease,
Eating unshelled peas,
Having arthritic knees.

Being locked out of your house,
Upsetting your spouse,
Crushing your computer mouse.

Narrowly missing your train,
Being caught in the rain,
Playing the Lotto in vain.

All these will never beat
The despond of defeat.

SONNET TO ENDEARMENT

I like the way you eat
Sugar lumps like a horse;
I like the way you treat
Me when I am off course.

I like the way you speak,
Mispronouncing words;
I like the way you tweak
And witter like the birds.

I like the way you care
When dealing with the old;
I like the way you share
The duvet when it's cold.

But what most endears is your smile,
Because it makes it all worthwhile.

SONNET TO ENTROPY

Scientists say that we don't matter –
We're insignificant and small.
But such words a fact don't shatter –
Individually, we are tall.

Infinity itself is hard to grasp:
A universe without limitation.
Morality is much simpler to clasp,
Though dying is no one's inclination.

What is irreconcilably dire
Is this timeless world and our fleeting lives,
Which makes important our blind desire
To ensure this thinking species survives.

It seems irrelevant why the earth spins;
Indeed, what counts is who loses or wins.

SONNET TO SELF-DEPRECATION

Arriving home Saturday night,
You looked lovely in your dress;
Then I learnt about your plight
And the shower room in a mess.

Recriminations came to a head,
With me to blame for stalling;
But rather than accept it as read,
You gave yourself a mauling.

Then you said that you're a Jonah,
When it's me who holds you back.
Perhaps in truth I'm a loner
Who finds it hard to share a track.

Though we are good for one another,
I'm no father, but you're a mother.

SONNET TO ORIENTATION

Forget Creation or evolution
As explanations of why I'm here;
What matters is dodging persecution
And keeping hold of all that's dear.

While humanity has many guises,
Expediency seems to be the key;
Thus life can have no surprises
Because the locksmith is you and me.

Hence good is what benefits my life,
And bad is what makes others suffer;
Their recourse is what can cause strife,
Yet do I relent or maybe get tougher.

So if you feel life's sold you short,
It's your own fault for being caught.

SONNET TO HANDICRAFT

Healing hands, fingers ready;
Healing hands, warm and steady.
Healing hands touch the skin;
Healing hands work within.

Healing hands stop the pain;
Healing hands ease the strain.
Healing hands soothe the nerves;
Healing hands, health preserves.

Healing hands help to unblock –
Healing hands – the body clock.
Healing hands calm the mind;
Healing hands, peace to find.

Healing hands impart belief
That healing hands will give relief.

SONNET TO DELINEATION

Whatever our hopes are while alive,
Our circumstances tend to lay the ground;
So even when we steadfastly strive,
Our hill can become a gigantic mound.

My reasoning may have gone astray,
But of my logic there is no doubt;
Existence is paved with tiles of grey
And it's for us to provide the grout.

Our influence in life may be small
And the parts we play can be overlooked,
So does it matter not standing tall
And knowing our value is undercooked?

With insight it was Keynes who said,
'In the long run, we are all dead.'

SONNET TO ELENCHUS

Is philosophy a worthy degree,
Or is it just an award in flim-flam?
The only difference that I can see
Is like that between gammon and ham.

Supposedly you're taught logic and reason,
So that problems can be analysed;
Yet it's common sense that's always in season
Without the need to be mesmerised.

Does existentialism matter a jot
Or does religion carry much weight?
Rhetorically, the answer is not,
For overthinking burdens our fate.

Since philosophy has no real claims,
Heed Hume and 'cast it to the flames'.

SONNET TO DETERIORATION

In my twenties squash became a habit,
An obsession fuelled by competition
To the exclusion of parturition,
Rushing about like a rabid rabbit.

Running helter-skelter like a ferret,
Chasing a squash ball around the court
In a manner that was self-taught,
Even winning some trophies on merit.

Many years later I'm like a toad,
Torpid in movement, in fact quite slow –
My mind says sprint, but my legs won't go,
As if I'm laden with a large load.

And now my hip has started playing up,
Leaving me feeling like a hamstrung tup!

SONNET TO DISQUIETUDE

If disaffection disturbs your heart,
Then consider this quite simple fact:
We are only here to play a part,
Regardless of how life is stacked.

Any displeasure that we may feel,
Or dissatisfaction harboured inside,
It remains with us to say, "No deal,"
Or else to launch ourselves with the tide.

Then if you think you cannot cope
Or come to terms with your standing,
There is no reason to lose hope –
Just make your aims less demanding.

While disappointment may arise,
Success can have no compromise.

PANEGYRICAL SONNET

Dave headed the Townley clan
And four fine children did he beget;
He was an upstanding man,
The best his wife, June, has ever met.

Being a lifelong Arsenal supporter
Did not lessen his popularity!
In fact, his stature grew no shorter
When others' views showed disparity.

Always ready to give his backing
To family and friends and worthy causes,
Dave's rectitude was never lacking;
His fortitude in life had no pauses.

Although struck down by an insidious disease,
His memory will remain as a calming breeze.

SONNET TO HAMARTIOLOGY

Theology can leave us wracked
With decisions that fill our life,
For it's easy to be sidetracked
Into steering away from strife.

Clearly there are rebarbative deeds
Which require swift condemnation;
But most of us can fulfil our needs
Without recourse to expiation.

Generally our behaviour's ingrained
With hortatory pleas for fair play,
So that venial actions are constrained
By the expediency of the day.

Sin is just a liminal idea –
It is ourselves, not God, that we fear.

SONNET TO PAGEANTRY

Forget the gloom and anxiety pills –
There's a royal wedding to celebrate.
Let's focus on Catherine and Wills
And the chance to become inebriate.

As if it mattered a single jot
That two pampered people come together!
Their liaison won't improve our lot,
Except for a day off – cue good weather.

Then when all the fuss has dissipated
And the parvenus have gone their way,
The marriage will soon be consummated
And for their issue, no doubt, we'll pay.

As an occasion it brings good cheer,
So maybe I'll buy a souvenir.

SONNET TO CONTRITION

I regret our relationship seems frayed
And unravelling at the edges;
However, please do not feel betrayed –
It's me who is poor on pledges.

Now that I've brought you to tears,
I don't think there's any way back;
It has just realised my fears
That we are not on the same track.

While my life I tend to derail,
There's no reason for you to abide;
After all, if bread becomes stale
You'd be the first to throw it outside.

Maybe we need to knead some fresh dough,
For it pains me to see your tears flow.

SONNET TO DEDICATION

Too often we think about life
As pointless and unredeeming;
But when we gauge the joy and strife,
We find with value it is teeming.

Such is the way for a mother
Whose devotion has no bound –
Always concern for another
To prevent them going aground.

A mother will voice her feeling
To assuage, reassure and advise,
Yet spurning her need for healing
While preserving familial ties.

If goodness is a measure of worth,
Then mothers are the salt of the earth.

SONNET TO MATRIMONY

We're here to cement our pairing
By formally tying the knot,
And to say that we'll be sharing
All we have – except for my yacht!

That includes all charges and chattels,
As well as contagious diseases;
Together we will face life's battles
And enjoy everything that pleases.

Now all that remains on our list
Is to thank you for attending;
And finally the bride can be kissed,
Although first my socks need mending!

So while now you may raise a glass to us,
Include Fate, because we met on a bus.

SONNET TO FICKLENESS

Who is to know what lies beneath
The public persona demonstrated?
Jimmy Savile's flowery wreath
Has not wilted, but he's castigated.

Likewise Lance Armstrong's now vilified
Because of allegedly taking drugs;
Yet no one complains when they're supplied
To counter cancer and virulent bugs.

Armstrong was an icon, Savile a saint,
Starting charities that benefit all;
Now their legacies will forever taint
Everyone's memory before their fall.

Yet why now the need for such expurgation
When gladly we marvelled their inspiration?

SONNET TO PROVIDENCE

This scroll is to be my final will
And a testament to my intent;
Completed, there'll be no need to fill
Another form to know what was meant.

If at any time I'm indisposed,
Non compos mentis – losing my mind –
Or become laid up and comatose,
Use no revival of any kind.

Thereafter all is left to my wife,
Except to Tony I leave my toys;
And if my organs can sustain life,
Donate them to prolong someone's joys.

Whatever is left, cremate me, please,
And decant the ashes on the breeze.

SONNET TO COSMOS

If there's a God,
Then He's a sod
For allowing people to suffer.
Yet endure they must,
Whether wrong or just –
For He's an indifferent duffer.

But if He's not there,
Then nothing's unfair
As nature takes its course:
It weeds out the frail
And coddles the hale
With its relentless force.

Calculated or not, whatever your views,
Life is a bomb that you cannot defuse.

SONNET TO ART

Does the artist exist to depict
Or is he there to portray?
Is it incumbent on him to inflict
The consciousness of the day?

Does a painter with an axe to grind
React against orthodox expression,
As the cubists, who sought to unwind
With a style representing aggression?

Does originality motivate art
And inspire us to celebrate life,
Or is it simply an arbitrary fart –
An exclamation of innate strife?

Art seeks to attain a second sight –
Surrealistically, we wish for flight.

SONNET TO SALLY

If there was a cat that could speak,
Then it's Sally I would nominate;
There's always a chirrup or squeak
And when alone she would ululate.

Regularly there'd be days
When a caterwaul would blare out;
Our attention this was to raise
And thereby allay any doubt.

When settled and secure she'd purr,
As most cats when curled on your lap;
But if anything disturbed her,
She'd chirp and then resume her nap.

For food there'd be a hankering wail
And a yelp if you trod on her tail!

SONNET TO ANNIVERSARY

"I told you not to smoke,
So now you have been sacked."
On my mum's words I choke
Because they were exact.

Despite my futile cusses,
Fate found another route:
Arriving on the buses,
Where soon I met a beaut.

One year we've now been married
With all that life can throw,
And together we have carried
A love I'm sure will grow.

Since paper represents one year,
This is all I could buy, my dear!

SONNET TO INSIGNIFICANCE

If I write as a non-believer,
It is to declaim our having souls;
For who would be a self-deceiver
By conceding that our lives have goals?

We're an agglomeration of senses
That are essentially flesh and blood,
In which case we can drop the pretences
That we're any more special than mud.

I'm not decrying that each of us counts
With an infrangible right to exist,
But with meaning our self-delusion mounts
Till our actions are ennoblingly kissed.

Thus life's transience is of no concern,
Nor afterwards will we regale or burn.

SONNET TO WHO

William Hartnell's monocle made him distinct
And Patrick Troughton had a recorder to play;
Jon Pertwee had a car called Bessie that winked,
While Tom Baker's long scarf was the talk of the day.

Peter Davison dressed as a cricket umpire,
Then Colin Baker flounced in a rainbow suit.
Sylvester McCoy shambled in garb that was dire,
While Paul McGann's Victorian togs looked cute.

Christopher Eccleston in leathers bossed the part,
While David Tennant doubled as a laid-back teacher.
Meanwhile Matt Smith's bow tie was as cool as a fart,
And now Peter Capaldi's Crombie is the feature.

What connects all the Doctors is quite plain –
Attractive companions to keep them sane.

SONNET TO REMORSE

Becks, I know I've been a chump,
Chasing someone so insincere,
Who in essence was just a frump
When all the time you were my peer.

My heart bleeds to know you're hurt
By my misconceived indiscretion;
Shamed indeed that I was so curt,
I'm undeserving of intercession.

I know in time our being is rooted
By what we feel to be our fate,
But so often it's convoluted –
We don't see truth until too late.

I fervently hope that time will heal,
For what we enjoyed was ethereal.

SONNET TO COGNITION

Our starting point is thought,
For without it we are nought;
But then, with it we are caught
Amid decisions which are fraught.

Thus we are invited to choose,
Based upon our differing views,
About everything that's in the news,
Deciding between the lies and truths.

Yet in fact what matters to most
Is whether we have a Sunday roast,
Confirming Juvenal's astute boast
That bread and circuses keep us engrossed.

While thinking serves to enhance our purpose,
Our limited choices make it seem surplus.

SONNET TO DECREPITUDE

Nearly sixty and not sitting pretty,
My decaying body's now in retreat;
Age is redeeming, but shows no pity
And will not change my cumbrous plates of meat.

Though genetics play an important part
In potential for physical prowess,
We will always be the jam on the tart
While the pastry below fails to impress.

Whoever affirmed 'age before beauty'
Did not compare Brucie with Kelly Brook;
There is no escape from Death's dread duty –
We are all eventually brought to book.

If only life could be lived in reverse,
Just so that the font could supplant the hearse.

SONNET TO REIFICATION

When the body ceases to function,
Then biologically we must be dead.
So why should we have some compunction
About perceptions that we leave unsaid?

While our thoughts can influence our mind
And our decisions ennoble our deeds,
It begs the question of where to find
The spirituality that life breeds.

Where is the basis for believing
That there's anything more beyond death?
For it's no more than self-deceiving
To conceptualise our last breath.

The sole consolation for devising a soul
Is the desolation of not having a goal.

SONNET TO ANGST

'Without faith, one cannot live'
Was Tolstoy's concise conclusion;
This followed his searching sieve
To sift out fact from illusion.

Even Dostoyevsky was quite blunt
In declaiming what we are about:
If God is just a specious front,
Then our actions would have no clout.

Yet our meaning does derive from deeds,
As existentialists like Sartre avow.
For self-validation surely breeds
The reasons for being in the here and now.

But, as Nagel noted, life is absurd –
A serious effort to polish a turd.

SONNET TO HOTCHPOTCH

Taoists think that all nature is one;
Baptists believe immersion is the key.
Jainists avow that no harm should be done,
While pagans prefer to worship a tree.

Monotheists abound in all but name –
Methodists, Catholics and C of E.
Maybe Muslims have a more righteous claim,
Or is Judaism what God did decree?

Hindus humour deities wrapped in mystique,
But Buddhists must walk an 'enlightened' path.
Sikhs and Shinto have a worthy critique,
While Witnesses peddle Jehovah's wrath.

The role of religion is to conceptualise
The meaning of life and its ultimate prize.

SONNET TO PEREGRINATION

It seemed that dog-walking was boring –
More for the dog than for me;
An exercise to stop her gnawing
And a chance for a liberal wee.

Then I encountered another
With a Labrador called Dex:
She was a delicious mother
In the posh version of text.

So pleasantries were swapped
About the weather and time of day,
But the conversation flopped
When her husband approached our way.

I thought dog-walking had a perk,
Yet I ended up being a berk.

SONNET TO INTERMISSION

The myth of Sisyphus should be dispelled
And seen as a truth we all enact,
For constantly in life we are propelled
To repeat ourselves, and that's a fact.

The glass half empty or the glass half full
Determines whether we curse our birth,
And when no longer wrapped in cotton wool
We begin to see what life is worth.

While routine confronts us in every way,
Interspersed with highlights of fun,
Inexorably we move towards the day
When finally no more can be done.

Footprints in time are all that we leave,
Just echoes of self with those that grieve.

SONNET TO MY MUSE

April 20th was the date
And Komedia, Bath, the place;
Once settled down, I couldn't wait
To glimpse Lulu's effulgent face.

Soon she skipped on to adoring roars,
And opened with 'Relight My Fire';
David Bowie's ballad brought applause,
Then 'Cry', with the Army Wives choir.

'To Sir, with Love' was plaintively sung,
As were her own compositions;
Then every note was vocally rung
From 'Shout!' without inhibitions.

And with the crescendo of sound,
Her brilliance again was crowned.

SONNET TO MORPHEUS

When dreaming have you noted
That you're not always in control?
It seems you're often outvoted
Or acting as if on parole.

You may be asleep and quite static,
But your dreams take you further afield,
Dropping you in scenes so dramatic
You are convinced that your fate is sealed.

People appear of their own volition,
Seemingly without invitation,
Then interact without precondition
Before you wake with consternation.

It seems when dreaming our minds are elsewhere,
Afloat in a soup of cosmic despair.

SONNET TO EPISTEMOLOGY

Logical thinking, so Leo Tolstoy thought,
Would negatively answer the query
That the meaning of life just amounts to nought
And would render existence less cheery.

Redemption for him came from changing tack
And taking a more subjective stance –
An outlook that Blaise Pascal might well back
By giving optimism a bigger chance.

Hence a belief that life has innate worth
Will countervail the mortality we face,
And the seeming pointlessness of our birth
Can then be dispelled by the dreams we all chase.

Fulfilment in life may be deemed a sham,
But it all depends on who gives a damn.

SONNET TO PERORATION

Schopenhauer thought life was something to suffer
Because of our constantly craving for stuff;
He has a point, the misanthropic duffer,
Since it appears we can never have enough.

He also believed life's devoid of meaning
Since it's daft for death to be its conclusion.
And anyone with a rational leaning
Would deduce its import as a delusion.

He also highlighted the irony of pain,
Since our body only speaks when it hurts;
But to live for its avoidance would be inane,
So we foist the pretence of just deserts.

The essence of life he worked to define
And saw his words strewn like pearls before swine.

SONNET TO EMBROILMENT

Being the President is a piece of cake,
Having a horde of advisors on tap,
Because even if you make a mistake
You know your entourage will take the rap.

Being the Pope is an invidious task,
Having to proselytise every day,
And then when you relax behind the mask
You're not allowed to get your end away.

Being the Queen is a walk in the park,
Presiding at functions with consummate ease,
But a fishbowl life must be quite stark
When continually part of a royal frieze.

Being the Dalai Lama is probably best,
Espousing your wisdom while half undressed.

SONNET TO AUTONOMY

Our lives are punctuated
With a diversity of choice,
But this is extirpated
When we don't have any voice.

So while we search for meaning
With each and every deed,
Unknowingly we're weaning
On a circumstantial creed.

Constrained by who we are,
Restricted by where we be,
Whether a pauper or a tzar,
It's important to be free.

So then potentially we can
Become the shepherd, not the lamb.

SONNET TO IMBROGLIO

The referendum was supposed to decide
The favoured route for Great Britain to thrive –
Whether the European courts should preside
Or our autonomy we could revive.

Should we be governed by Maastricht muppets
And be told how to control our borders,
Or cease being their obedient puppets
And defy their derivative orders?

Should our trading with all be precluded,
With our Parliament subjected to theirs;
And is this single market deluded
Into thinking it answers *our* prayers?

The supreme irony having voted to leave –
We're negotiating to keep what did aggrieve!

SONNET TO FIXATION

We're all able to make our choices –
To place ourselves in situations,
And listen to our inner voices
Regarding all the permutations.

But with some things we have no control,
Like circumstances others may lay;
In which case it may seem like parole
Until our input can seize the day.

So whatever it seems will be our lot,
The starting point is knowing who we are;
But now those unhappy with what they've got
Can physically change like jam in a jar.

'The mind is its own place,' Milton famously said;
So when it comes to gender, it's all in the head.

SONNET TO DISCOMFITURE

When all is said and done
And your play has had its run,
Only echoes will remain.

When the chickens are home to roost
And now nothing has you goosed,
You can sense you're on the wane.

When the banquet has been devoured
And the aftertaste leaves you soured,
Your sunshine soon turns to rain.

When your cards have all been played
And you think you've made the grade,
You wonder if it's all in vain.

Yet beyond the harsh truth of ageing,
Within you life's fire keeps on raging.

SONNET TO DISTRACTION

Voicing your views, having a say,
Voting for people on display;
Britain's Got Talent paves the way,
Allowing some to have their day.

A royal wedding also provides
Some national cheer that overrides
The republican–monarchy divides,
Until eventually it all subsides.

The football World Cup foments feeling
When a win begins the healing,
Then the Germans send us reeling
And with reality soon we're dealing.

Routine supplants the brief diversions
Until we're offered more excursions.

SONNET TO PERTINENCE

Living in the West
We are really obsessed
And concerned with what we eat;

Knowing what is best
To safely ingest
With a diet we have to meet.

Meanwhile children are obese
With burgers fried in grease
And lush milkshakes overly sweet;

This so parents get peace
While their kids' bodies they lease
To junk food with sugar replete.

Even Jamie Oliver can't complain
While making cheesecake that's inhumane!

SONNET TO DENOUEMENT

It was God who allegedly said,
"Alpha and Omega – that's who I am."
And for our sins His only Son bled,
Or is it just an elaborate scam?

The Epistles, after all, are someone's word
About history purportedly made;
How do we know what actually occurred,
Since it's easy for the truth to be frayed?

If the Bible is gospel and taken as fact,
Then evolution is a non-starter;
But one thing this theory patently lacked –
Darwinians never produced a martyr.

Logic suggests life is a one-way street,
Yet mortality leaves us incomplete.

SONNET TO MACHINATION

We're political beasts, Aristotle said,
Enabling us to secure our rights;
But because we are so easily led,
We become like moths drawn to the lights.

The right to life and freedom to speak
Are both dependent on our actions.
But those unheard are deemed to be weak
And dominated by louder factions.

Self-determination may be our goal,
But it's only achieved through group debate.
Ultimately the world decides our role
According to how we choose to relate.

We accommodate ourselves the best we can
With expediency underwriting our plan.

SONNET TO DEFLATION

I remember starting my first job –
A solicitor's clerk in the city.
I was told to go earn a few bob
And not to stay home bathing in pity.

Decked in a swish suit my mother bought
And a subsidy to cover my fare,
A London Underground train I caught,
Arriving early with time to spare.

Feeling self-important, I lit a fag
And sauntered past Fortnum to Jermyn Street.
On being shown my 'office', my head did sag –
It was filled with crockery, all piled neat.

It then became quite clear to me,
I was employed to make the tea!

SONNET TO UNFULFILMENT

Ever since the heroes of '66,
English football has been bogged in a mire,
Invariably losing on penalty kicks,
Until exorcised by Eric Dyer.

With Tunisia beaten at the death,
And Panama taken to the cleaners,
Belgium was used as a chance to draw breath
Before Colombian misdemeanours.

In the quarter-finals young Pickford shone
As Sweden succumbed to some measured play;
But then with Croatia our luck was done
And our dreams dispelled for another day.

So kudos to Southgate and not the sack,
But that damn monkey is still on his back!

World Cup, 2018

SONNET TO FASCINATION

Sixty miles above us is darkness and cold,
A vacuum of interminable space;
And lying beyond, a universe untold
And dwarfing us, the petty human race.

On a global scale we are merely specks
Busying ourselves in ignorant bliss,
For our existence relies upon the checks
That the cosmos isn't just hit and miss.

The Goldilocks theory applies to our earth,
Where all is just right for us to exist,
Yet we take for granted humanity's birth
And on the planet have become a cyst.

Our oasis of life should be celebrated
And not despoiled by what we have perpetrated.

SONNET TO PURPOSE

If anything you do has a reason,
Then your motivation is fulfilled;
But if your life lacks all cohesion,
Then perchance your aims should be distilled.

Satisfying needs is the bottom line,
Craving attention or being recognised;
Excelling somehow allows you to shine
And being academic is also prized.

But generally speaking we all exist
With most of us living from hand to mouth;
Only the privileged compile a list,
Like surgery to stop their boobs going south!

Such disparities are nobody's fault,
It's just some are born pepper, others salt.

SONNET TO PATER

You are a really special dad
Because you have always cared;
You cheer me up when I am sad
And calm me if I am scared.

Early on you helped me to speak
When I had trouble with my diction;
Such devotion makes you unique
In conquering such an affliction.

You brought us up to show respect
And treat others as you have shown.
In all you do you are correct
And so are we now we have flown.

All in all you are the bee's knees –
Ever eager to try and please.

SONNET TO PROCRASTINATION

I wake up early with nothing to do
And I've got the whole day to do it;
In retrospect I'd not thought it through
Because I had my chance and blew it.

Opportunity knocks for one and all,
So get up and answer the door;
Whatever you do you shouldn't forestall
And think of life as one long chore.

You would be up and about in a shot
If something without effort were needed.
After all, fruit that's not ripened will rot
And no wheat will grow unless it's seeded.

So it's not enough to boil the kettle –
James Watt did more and thus showed his mettle.

SONNET TO DYSPHORIA

The malaise of modern life is clear:
We have too much time on our hands,
Forever looking for something to cheer
Because we've lost our place in the stands.

It's all about satisfying our needs
And the frustration of their pursuit.
Then soon we become like stifling weeds
And incapable of bearing fruit.

So now self-realisation is key
And God's purpose can now be our own;
No longer blinkered by what we see,
Our factitious desires are fully grown.

It seems to consumption we are enslaved,
When all along it was freedom we craved.

SONNET TO VACILLATION

Are we in Europe or are we out?
The referendum decided we leave;
But "Just a minute," I hear you shout:
"Remainers are looking for a reprieve."

Should we jettison our continent ties
And rely on garnering global trade?
Yet remainers say we were peddled lies
To undo the Maastricht promise we made.

The majority want borders protected
From all and sundry coming willy-nilly;
The minority claim those we've elected
Say excluding migrants would be silly.

The Brexit problem is up in the air,
So where will it land? Does anyone care!

SONNET TO LETHE

When soldiering was considered an art,
There was a clash of swords or a pistol duel;
Chivalry also played a gallant part
Because being a poltroon would never be cool.

Then kings and rulers began to hold sway,
Fighting battles to gain riches and land;
For all that mattered at the close of day
Was 'might is right', so all could understand.

This gave rise to patriotic passion,
Where people are beholden to the state;
So wars ensued like they're out of fashion
Involving millions without wish to hate.

In history the perpetrators are written,
But never forget those valiantly smitten. . . .

SONNET TO CONSANGUINITY

Who said that life is unfair
Or that we should even care –
Perhaps we should.

Who said that love carries the day
And overshadows all affray –
Perhaps it could.

Who said that prayer is futile
And not able to raise a smile –
Perhaps it would.

Who said we are on borrowed time
While listening to Big Ben chime –
Perhaps that's good.

So, when all is said and done,
Perhaps we'll see that life is fun.

SONNET TO INTROSPECTION

My inspiration has now sapped;
My resource has me vacated.
My vocabulary has been tapped
And with these poems I'm placated.

From my thoughts I have extrapolated
That for some I hold the highest esteem;
And I've learnt that being infatuated
Differs from love like milk does from cream.

Of this earthly life, I have concluded
That it's a trial of personal adaptation,
Where it's easy for us to be deluded
Into losing sight of our destination.

In verse I've extricated my emotions
And thus I have seen my inner notions.